Advance Praise for *Each Journey Begins With a Single Step*

In this compendium of translations from the *Daodejing (Tao Te Ching)*, the *Yijing (I Ching)*, Chinese proverbs, the *Book of Rites*, *Analects*, the poetry of Wang Wei, Li Bai, Du Fu, and others, Deng Ming-Dao has given us a great wisdom book of Chinese philosophy and poetry, of political values and religious thought. At the center of the book is the Tao, a way of seeing and a way of being. Deng Ming-Dao's masterful translations demonstrate what mindfulness is. This is a book to keep near and to savor, to return to again and again, each page a step into the journey.

—**Joe Stroud**, author of *In the Sleep of Rivers; Signatures; Below Cold Mountain; Country of Light;* and *Of This World: New and Selected Poems*

Deng Ming-Dao is a canny, discerning guide through the deep wisdom contained in the foundational texts of Chinese thought and philosophy. Rendered in lustrous and compelling new translations, Deng here offers readers the complete *Daodejing* interspersed with complementary selections from the *Yijing*, the *Analects*, the *Book of Rites*, as well as Chinese poems, proverbs, and treatises. From these many sources, Deng has assembled a compelling tapestry, a subtle and lucid compendium that can be read as a map, though it leads to no preordained destination. A sage fellow traveler, Deng knows that the journey is all, and with *Each Journey Begins With a Single Step* he offers his heart and his hand to anyone who would follow the same road. This book is a precious gem—a gift to anyone who would "follow the Tao for life."

—**Gary Young**, author of *Hands; The Dream of a Moral Life; Days; Braver Deeds; No Other Life; Pleasure; Bear Flag Republic: Prose Poems and Poetics from California;* and *Even So: New and Selected Poems*

A marvelously engaging and innovative omnibus! Deng Ming-Dao maps here the way of China's perennial philosophies. A wise and trusty mentor, he lets the landscape, within us all and all around us, speak for itself, so that we may each find our own way with this timeless guide.

—**Gary Gach**, author of *Pause, Breathe, Smile*

The poeticality and spiritual depth of Deng Ming-Dao's writing inspires the reader to believe that wisdom will save humanity from self-destruction. The Taoist artist's translation of the *Daodejing* and other ancient Chinese works provides a new and thought-provoking approach to the Truth, known and still unknown . . .

—**Larisa Segida**, author of *Berries: 210 Thoughts and Photographs on Life, Love and Light*

As a poet, I appreciate the complexity, simplicity, and mystery of these verses. As a man who devoted a great deal of his life to athletics, I was moved profoundly by the physical and organic nature of the imagery. "I bare my chest to the living clouds/strain my eyes toward the birds flying home/I will climb to the very summit/and shrink many mountains within a single glance." When I read from "The Song of Practicing the Thirteen Dynamics," from *Shanxi Wang Zongye's Taijiquan Treatise*, I thought these words should be compulsory reading for every aspiring athlete. There is great wisdom in this collection. Deng Ming-Dao's translations need to be kept at one's bedside for reading before sleep and for reading the moment one awakes. One could not end the day or begin the day in a better way.

—**Tom Meschery**, author of *Over the Rim; Caught in the Pivot: The Diary of a Rookie Coach in the Exploding World of Pro Basketball; Nothing We Lose Can Be Replaced; Some Men; Sweat: New and Selected Poems About Sports*

Each Journey Begins With a Single Step

Each Journey Begins With a Single Step

The Taoist Book of Life

SELECTED, TRANSLATED, AND EDITED BY

Deng Ming-Dao

HAMPTON ROADS

Cover design by Deng Ming-Dao

Cover image: *Dream Journey among Rivers and Mountains,* Number 150, by Cheng Zhengkui (1604–1676). Dated 1662. Handscroll, ink and color on paper. Overall including mount, 36.8 x 921.7 cm. Los Angeles County Museum of Art.

Interior image: *Remote View of Streams and Hills,* by Xia Gui (fl. 1195–1224). Handscroll, ink on paper, 46.5 x 889.1 cm. National Palace Museum, Taipei, Taiwan.

Interior design by Deng Ming-Dao

Typeset by Side By Side Studios, San Francisco, CA

Hampton Roads Publishing Company, Inc.
Charlottesville, VA 22906
Distributed by Red Wheel/Weiser, LLC

www.redwheelweiser.com

SIGN UP FOR OUR NEWSLETTER AND SPECIAL OFFERS BY GOING TO *WWW.REDWHEELWEISER.COM/NEWSLETTER.*

ISBN: 978-1-57174-838-6

Library of Congress Cataloging-in-Publication Data available upon request.

Printed in Canada

MAR

10 9 8 7 6 5 4 3 2 1

Contents

Introduction

In the sixth century BCE, an imperial archivist, philosopher, and teacher named Laozi decided to leave his declining country. Within fifty years, his homeland would be consumed as seven major and four minor states fought to conquer one another. The ensuing 254 years of intrigues and battles gave the era its name: the Warring States (475–221 BCE).

Records tell us that Laozi, whose name literally means "Old Master," was wise enough that Confucius himself discussed philosophy with him. Both men worked to define the right ways of living and governance. However, the two men had different approaches. Confucius believed in the rites; he wanted to bring order through a system of rigid social relationships. In contrast, Laozi believed in Tao—meaning the Way; he felt that society was intrusive and that it distorted human purity. People should instead follow a natural and simple way of life. Both men strived for peace and order even as their country fell apart. Confucius responded to this by trying to find a ruler who would put his ideas into practice. Laozi , who wrote "know when enough is enough," withdrew from his responsibilities, mounted a water buffalo, and rode the many miles to the western border. That was the edge of the civilized world as he knew it. Only vast mountains and plains sparsely populated with nomadic tribes lay beyond the border.

At the garrison pass, a guard named Yinxi recognized Laozi. He begged the great teacher to leave a record of his wisdom. In response, Laozi wrote the *Daodejing* and instructed this last disciple before he rode through the fortified gates.

In that book, Laozi wrote the famous line, "A journey of a thousand miles begins with a single step." What must he have been thinking as he went into the wilderness? What compassion did he show for Yinxi, and, by extension, all who read his book, that he paused before taking this last journey? He clearly meant his words as a guide, because he knew that generations of people would follow him.

That's how we step outside each day as we journey through a world of unknowns. In this, we are not just like Laozi; we are like every human being since the beginning of our species. We walk on the same earth, where nothing else is lower or deeper than the ground. We raise our heads to the same sky above, where nothing else is higher or farther than the heavens. This is our entire world. If we are to find guidance, it will be on the road.

Each day, we feel the winds that stir the air we breathe. We drink water that flows from springs and wells, rivers and lakes. We seek heat when the weather is cold, and we cook our food over fire. When we walk, gravity anchors our bodies to this grand planet. During the day, the sun warms us, gives us the light to see, and casts the shadows that show us shape and volume. During the night, we mark the months and seasons by the moon, and we navigate by the stars. We have the same heart, breath, body, and mind as every other person we meet, as every person before us has had, and as every person after us will have. And yet, each of us is our own person, with our own feelings and ideas, and our own wills and hopes. We are both the same as everyone else and yet different.

The ancients observed this paradox. Perhaps they would put it this way: we are all human, and yet each of us has individual obligations. There are good, but not immediately apparent, ways to have a fulfilled life. Confucius and Laozi, along with the poets, philosophers, noble ones (cultivated persons), and recluses, left us their wisdom in our own searches.

The vital stream of their combined thoughts goes back to the beginnings of recorded history in China. With a calendar that began in 2637 BCE, the earliest preserved document that dates from the *Canon of Emperor Yao* (c. 2356– 2255 BCE), a great body of literature in the Three Teachings (Taoism, Confucianism, Buddhism), and some of the best poems in the world, this stream offers us a tremendous advantage. We need only read their words.

As we examine these texts, we can't help but be conscious of the words themselves. Chinese ideographs are derived from pictures. Even abstract ideas are based on images of the world: sky, earth, water, fire, mountains, trees, river, lakes, ocean, rock, wind, plants, animals, insects, birds, people. While the language developed in complexity and extended meanings, it remained rooted in these observations. Tangibility was preferred. The writers spoke in terms of what they saw, heard, smelled, tasted, and touched. When it came time to speak of a world in constant flux, they summarized their observation with one word: *Tao.**

The written word for Tao shows a person, in the form of a head, pictured as 首 . That symbol is combined with the sign for walking: 辶 . (The sign was originally written as 辵 , which is a symbol for feet.) Tao is a person walking. Since the head also represents a chief, it can also imply a person leading us on a path.

Over the centuries this visual metaphor was loaded with many meanings:

> *Way, road, or path:* This is the trail to which the leader brings us. By extension, it came to mean the trail itself. The leader may not be present, but the way remains.

> *Direction:* Generally, you can go one of two ways on a long path. Choosing the right direction is important, and so Tao can simply refer to that.

> *Principle, truth,* or *reason:* If we learn how to walk in the right direction on a good path, we'll discover the prin-

---

* *Tao* and *dao* are both transliterations of the same word. *Tao* is more recognized in English and so it is used as its own standalone term. *Dao* is the accurate romanization according to current but newer usage.

ciple, truth, and reason we should walk that path. We'll learn why. When we learn why, it tells us something we can extrapolate to all paths.

Say, speak, talk, questions, commands: If leaders grasp the principles and are responsible for teaching or leading, then they have to speak, explain, persuade, ask and answer questions, and give commands.

Method, skill, steps in a process: Once principles are codified, they can be utilized and engineered. New paths are possible if one has a method. With a method repeatedly followed, skill develops.

Tao is just one word out of an estimated 23,000–90,000 characters. Most of them have multiple meanings. That makes reading, let alone translating, a delicious process of relishing many possible interpretations. We aren't reading words as if they are bricks, mortared by grammar into a single linear thought. We are viewing pictures as a collection of scenes with a web of rich associations between them.

Poetry became the ideal form for such a visual language. Freed from the restrictions of prose, Chinese poetry frequently dispensed with any subject-verb-object structure. Introductory explanations of a scene were often omitted. This keeps us in pure experience. The natural scenes become more than the setting for the story. The undeniability of nature supports the poem's truth.

When Tao is the subject, we are given the essence as quickly as possible. We are not being *told* of Tao. We are with the poet, seeing, hearing, and feeling the same things at the same time.

The possibilities of multiple meanings are apparent in the famous opening line of the *Daodejing*: "The Tao that can be said is not the constant Tao." If you look at the original Chinese, you can see that we've had to add words to make the line intelligible. Linguistically, however, the line seems constructed to tell us a plethora of things at once, implying other possibilities.

道 可 道 ， 非 常 道

The line can be read nearly as a mathematical formula:

道 Tao + 可 [may, can, -able; possibly] + 道 Tao + 非 [not, negative, non-; oppose] + 常 [common, normal, frequent, regular] + 道 Tao.

You could insert any number of meanings for Tao into the three places where it appears in this line, combine that with any of the meanings of the other words, and make a number of reasonable interpretations. If you also consider that we approach everything with our own subjectivity, you can see why we can't demand that the poetry of Tao tell us "just one thing." Instead, it really tells us "our thing." It allows us to take our own meaning from the lines.

The ideographs are also symbols for sound. Spoken Chinese is a tonal language that can be lovely and melodic. Generally, each basic sound has one of five tones that are either a rising, a falling, or a neutral tone. Ritual chanting of poetic scripture was a significant form of Taoism, and it is still practiced today. For these devotees, the words have power. To possess the writings is to hold the sacred. To chant the words is to listen to Tao. To feel that resonance purifies and integrates the chanter with Tao. (Our words *enchantment* and *chant* have the same roots.)

As the culture evolved, the words took on an elevated significance. For example, nine tripod cauldrons cast from tribute bronze from nine provinces were made by order of Yu the Great (c. 2200–2101 BCE) and meticulously engraved; possessing them was considered a sign of legitimacy for subsequent dynasties. Imperial inscriptions carved into enormous stone stelae survive from as early as the third century BCE. In the Han Dynasty, the Xiping Stone Classics were installed at the Imperial Academy outside Luoyang in 175–183. The seven classics (including the *Yijing*) comprised about 200,000 characters, and they were carved on forty-six stelae. The poem "Climbing Xian Mountain Together with Friends" (p. 16) centers on a visit to a stela and indicates the deep admiration that was felt for such stone tablets. Even today, you can see inscriptions chiseled into the cliffs of famous sites, turning the landscapes into gigantic paintings with poetic inscriptions. The writing, which originated as pictures, took on its own presence in the world.

This brings us to the combination of Chinese painting and poetry that existed for more than a thousand years. That was made possible by the flexible but pointed brush used by craftspeople, artists, and writers alike. Literati paintings from as early as the Yuan Dynasty (1271–1368) were inscribed with at least one poem. If words like *Tao* were formed by combining two symbols, effectively creating a new metaphor, combining pictures and words extended the layers of imagery.

In the majority of cases, both the poetry and paintings remained grounded in nature. Many of the poems in this book open with a natural scene, and philosophical concepts are couched in terms of tangible things. When Laozi tells us of the central concept of nothingness, he speaks in terms of a cart wheel, a bowl, doors, and windows (p. 167). Wang Wei, who was also a devout Buddhist, may ultimately be telling us about meditation, but he opens with a leisurely description of the Massed Fragrance Temple and mountain forests (p. 81). When it comes to the paintings themselves, they are often dramatic landscapes of sheer mountains, old pines, and splashing waterfalls. There might be a traveler or a pair of friends in one corner of the painting, tiny in the vast wilderness. Usually, we're told that this represents people's insignificance in the enormity of nature. But what if this is simply a frank statement of how human beings are a part of nature, and how a person is more than a body, but is also inseparable from their surroundings? What if showing a human being is also to acknowledge their journey? To convey that, then, demanded a depiction that unified words, calligraphy, painting, and spoken language.

Let's return to Laozi, sitting in a garrison on the frontier. He wrote of the Way and its Power with ideographs that were in themselves images of the world. He made a book of pictographs that ask us to simply be present in this world. He then went into that world forever, leaving a trail of word-pictures so that we could follow.

This book looks at his words and thoughts, and then goes on to juxtapose those with many other poets who give their own views and recounted their personal experiences. Three major sources are worth mentioning. The first is the *Daodejing.* A complete translation of that classic is here, although it's been rearranged to alternate with other views. The second is the *Yijing,* particularly the section known as the Images, said to have been written by Confucius. The third is the Chinese poetic tradition itself. Many of the poets were spiritual aspirants, and their viewpoints are valuable. A large number of poems are drawn from the anthology *300 Tang Poems;* many consider these poems the best in all of Chinese history. Occasionally, there are words or names of people that either will leave a person curious or have meanings that will greatly enhance the reading of a poem. A glossary and further notes about major bibliographic sources are at the end of this book.

The poems and chapters are arranged to form a journey. The first chapter, "Journey," gives observations about the venture itself. "Beginnings" is there because every journey must start properly. "Beyond Names" reminds us that we are pursuing more than what we can label. "Yin Yang" explains the fundamental forces underlying all that we experience. Some of those experiences are sad, but the testaments of those who have gone before us is valuable; that's why we have the chapter titled "Sorrow." Pain often turns us back to "Seeking," and inevitably, we will reflect on the "Cycles" that lead us through both good and bad fortune.

All of that together is "Tao," a path leading through "Heaven and Earth." While that's the whole world, the truth about that is "Mystery." We can best deal with that by being "Soft." We have to pursue "Excellence." We have to engage in "Self-Cultivation." But what do we aim for? We aim for "Sageliness" and "Peace." As we reach toward the spiritual, we'll understand natural effort, which is called "Nonaction." We'll realize the power of emptiness and that it's important to realize the power of "Nothingness." There is only the journey. There is no destination. There is only "Simplicity."

We walk the Way each day. We don't know what's ahead, but we can follow the wisdom of others. They speak of the joys, griefs, and purity in life. Like good pathfinders, they give us direction and prepare us, and then they encourage us to walk for ourselves. Let us take their words as our companion for every step of our thousand-mile journey.

1

旅行

Journey

1

A journey of a thousand miles
begins with a single step.

Daodejing 64

2

One heart.
One mind.

Proverb

3

Gongsun Yang said:
"To doubt the journey is to achieve nothing.
To doubt one's work is to accomplish nothing."

Book of Lord Shang, "Reform of the Law"

4

This temple: I remember traveling here once.
I recall this bridge that I now cross again.
Rivers and mountains seem to have been waiting,
flowers and willows have been more than unselfish.
The countryside shines vividly through thin mist,
the soft sun on the sand is the color of dusk.
All of this traveler's sorrows fade away.
Why should I leave this place again?

"Traveling Again," Du Fu (712–770)

旅
行

5

Who can describe this Great Peak?
The province is not yet green,
yet nature gathers its divine beauty
and yin parts from yang at dusk and dawn.
I bare my chest to the living clouds,
strain my eyes toward the birds flying home.
I will climb to the very summit
and shrink many mountains within a single glance.

"Gazing at the Peak," Du Fu (712–770)

6

The heavy is the root of the light.
Stillness is the ruler of agitation.

That is why the wise journey all day,
    but never stray from their supply carts.
They may have glorious views,
    but they pass them over
    and settle themselves comfortably instead.

How can the lords of ten thousand chariots
carry themselves lightly through the world?
    If they are light, they lose their roots.
    If they are agitated, they lose rulership.

Daodejing 26

旅
行

7

Following wind
is the image of mildness.
A noble one gives commands
and sets all matters in motion.

Yijing, Image of hexagram 57: Wind

8

Heaven will never take away a person's road.

Proverb

9

Heavy dampness, moving dew.
Should I walk here this morning?
But a journey means much dew.

Classic of Poetry, "Moving Dew"

10

A bottle of clear rice wine worth ten thousand coins.
Ten thousand dollars for delicacies on a jade dish.
I stop drinking, throw cup and chopsticks overboard,
and can eat no more. I draw my sword,
and look wildly around, my heart at a loss.
I want to cross the Yellow River, but the waters are iced.
I'd climb the Taihang Mountains, but snow blots out the
   sky.
I would sit and fish idly at a blue creek, but then
I'm suddenly back in my boat, dreaming at the edge of the
   sun.
The road is hard! The road is hard!
Too many forks in this road! Which one is right?
It must be possible to ride the wind and crest the waves,
and set sail where clouds hang over the endless seas!

"The Hard Road, 1," Li Bai (701–762)

11

Thunder in the sky above
is the image of great vigor.
A noble one never walks
toward the improper.

Yijing, Image of hexagram 34: Great Vigor

旅行

12

The monk from Shu carries his qin, "Green Silk,"
on his way down Mount Emei's western slope.
He'll work his hands simply for my sake:
it's like hearing a valley of ten thousand pines.

Flowing water washes this traveler's heart,
resonance spreads from frosted bells.
I'm unaware of sunset in the blue mountains,
and how much is hidden by thick autumn clouds.

"The Monk from Shu Plays His Qin," Li Bai (701–762)

13

A mountain lake
is the image of fullness.
A noble one openly
accepts others.

Yijing, Image of hexagram 31: Fullness

14

When three people walk together,
One of them can certainly teach me.

Analects, "Shu Er"

15

Toward a thatched roof on the mountain top:
I climbed straight up thirty miles,
knocked on the gate— no acolyte came.
Peeked in your room—little but a table.

Have you gone out in your rustic cart?
Are you fishing in autumn's clear waters?
We have missed seeing each another—
was it just empty effort to reach this spot?

The green grass is bright in the new rain,
the pines stir, hamlet windows are shuttered.
This moment, I give myself over to serenity,
content to let my whole heart be cleansed.

I arrived here without an idea
of how to find the essence of tranquility,
I can descend the mountain directly now:
there's no need to wait for a master.

"Seeking the Recluse of West Mountain and Not Finding Him,"
Qiu Wei (694–789?)

16

Return to your own Way.
How can this be wrong?

> *Yijing*, Line 1 of hexagram 9: The Little Tames

17

This morning my office is cold.
I've neglected my mountain friend
who gathers firewood by the high streams,
and returns to cook over white stones.
I'd like to bring you a ladle of wine,
go far to cheer you in stormy nights.
But dead leaves heap the bare slopes:
where would I ever find your trail?

> "Sent to Taoist Priest Zhong of Quanjiao Mountain,"
> Wei Yingwu (737–792)

18

Wind blowing above the earth
is the image of beholding.
The ancient kings toured the provinces
to see the people and display the teachings.

> *Yijing*, Image of hexagram 20: Beholding

19

Take a step to see the next step.

> Proverb

20

Morning rain in Wencheng dampens rising dust.
Sprouting willows color the guest house green.
Sir, let us drain another cup of wine.
Once you're west of Yang Gate, you'll have no friends.

> "Seeing Yuan Er Off on a Mission to Anxi," Wang Wei (699–759)

21

Leaves fall. Geese fly south.
The north wind blows. The river freezes.
My home is where the Xiang River bends.
Distant and far, Chu is high in the clouds.
I used up my homesick tears while traveling.
I see a single sail on the horizon.
Losing my way, I have to ask directions:
the sea is flat, the evening is without end.

> "Pondering Early Cold on the River," Meng Haoran
> (689/691–740)

22

A good traveler leaves
    neither wheel ruts nor footprints.
A good speaker is flawless
    and can't be reproached.
A good reckoner
    needs no calculators.
A well-shut door needs no bolts
    yet can't be opened.
A good knot uses no rope
    and can't be untied.

      Daodejing 27

23

Think three times—then move.

      Proverb

24

Walk the calm and level Way.
The recluse is pure. Good fortune.

      Yijing, Line 2 of hexagram 10: Walking

2 Beginnings

始

25

If we find the old Tao
that drives what we have today,
we can find the primal beginning.
    That is called the tradition of Tao.

Daodejing 14

26

Water added to the lake
is the image of regulation.
A noble one sets number and measure
and speaks of virtuous action.

Yijing, Image of hexagram 60: Regulation

27

Even when the chariot is before a mountain,
there will be a road.

Proverb

28

Tao birthed One.
One birthed Two.
Two birthed Three.
Three birthed the ten thousand things.

Daodejing 42

始

29

There's no "One" that cannot be divided.
No "Two" that does not have two names.
Find someone who can drink up the whole West River
and they can explain Tao to you.

"Not One, Not Two," Badashanren (1626–1705)

30

The supreme ultimate is born from the limitless
that is the mother of the ten thousand things.
It divides in movement.
It combines in stillness.
It never goes to excess:
it follows, bends, engages, and extends.

Shanxi Wang Zongyue's Taijiquan Treatise

31

From the beginning,
these have had the One:
    Heaven had one purity.
    Earth had one stability.
    Gods had one spirit.
    Valleys had one fullness.
    All the creatures had one life.
    Princes and kings only had one
    mode of integrity in the world.

And so,
if heaven did not have purity,
    it would break fearfully.
If earth had no stability,
    it would quake fearfully.
If the gods lacked spirit
    they would falter fearfully.
If valleys never filled,
    they would be drained fearfully.
If the creatures had no life,
    they would perish fearfully.
If the princes and kings had no integrity
    they would topple fearfully.

Daodejing 39

32

Have a beginning, have an end:
that would be sagely!

Analects, Zi Zhang

始

33

Heaven and earth clashing
is the image of dispute.
A noble one plans the right start
for all matters.

Yijing, Image of hexagram 6: Dispute

34

I urge you: don't covet clothes of golden threads.
I urge you: cherish your youthful years.
Pick the flowers as soon as they're on the branch.
Don't wait until that branch is bare to the touch.

"Clothes of Golden Threads," Du Qiuniang (d. 825?)

35

Walking forward in austerity is without blame.

Yijing, Line 1 of hexagram 10: Walking

36

The world had a beginning,
which was the mother of the world.

If we know the mother,
  then we know the children.
Once we know the child,
  we should, in turn, guard the mother.

Then none will be harmed.

Daodejing 52

37

Grieved and sad to leave my friends,
I'll drift and float in the fog
back to my post in crowded Luoyang.
Brutally the Guangling bell rings out,
signaling for me to leave at dawn.
Worldly cares storm every boat:
follow the stream to live in peace.

"Embarking on the Yangzi, Sending a Letter to Officer Yuan,"
Wei Yingwu (737–792)

3 無名 Beyond Names

38

The names that can be named,
  are not the constant names.

Daodejing 1

39

I walked a single path to where you lived,
and found a footprint in the moss.

White mists surround a quiet island.
The idle gate is overgrown with spring grass.

After the rain, the pines are a deeper green.
Following the mountain, I reach the water source.

Creek flowers for a meditative mind:
facing them, I have no need for words.

"Searching Nanxi for the Reclusive Changshan Taoist,"
Liu Changqing (710?–789?)

40

The origin of heaven and earth has no name.
Names are the Mother of the ten thousand things.

Daodejing 1

無名

41

Too much speech counts for little.
Don't compare; guard the middle.

Daodejing 5

42

Human affairs follow one after another:
coming, going, and completing, from past to present.
    Rivers and mountains endure in splendid place,
    and we return to visit them again and again.
Beyond rapids, fish swim in shallows by a bridge;
the cold sky is like a dream in a deep pool.
    Here is General Yang's stele with its inscription.
    Once we read it, our tears soak our gowns.

"Climbing Xian Mountain Together with Friends," Meng Haoran
(689/691–740)

43

One word can be worth a thousand pieces of gold.

> Proverb

44

Thunder beneath the mountain
is the image of nourishing.
A noble one is guarded in speech
and moderate in food and drink.

> *Yijing*, Image of hexagram 27: Nourishing

無名

45

Red leaves, a gloomy and sad night.
This long pavilion, a ladle of wine.
The clouds part: I would return to Taihua
where rain showers cross its dividing center.
Trees color the distant slopes green.
Rivers resound to the far-away seas.
I will reach the imperial city tomorrow
but I dream of being a fisherman or woodsman.

> "On an Autumn Day, Inscribed at Tongguan Staging Post on My
> Way to the Capital," Xu Hun (791–858)

46

Heaven and earth join as one
and send down sweet dew
to everyone evenly
without anyone's command.

Once that starts, it has a name.
Once it is named,
then people know to stay in it.
Once they know to stay in it,
they know no danger.

The Tao in this world,
can be compared
to streams running in gullies,
turning into rivers
coursing to the seas.

Daodejing 32

47

When drinking water, think of the source.

Proverb

無名

48

Wind blowing from fire by itself
is the image of a family.
A noble one is true in speech
and constant in deed.

Yijing, Image of hexagram 37: Family

無名

49

A clear creek of unmeasured depth.
A lone retreat hidden in clouds.
A row of dewy pines, a faint moon:
its pure light beams onto you.
Flower shadows dapple a thatched hut
and a courtyard patterned thick with herbs.
So much! I'm grateful to pass the time:
crane and phoenix flock to the western hills.

"Lodging for the Night at Wang Changling's Retreat,"
Chang Jian (708–765)

50

If you don't want people to know, don't do it.

Proverb

51

Fire on the mountain
is the image of the traveler.
A noble one is clear and cautious
when giving punishment
and yet does not delay trial.

Yijing, Image of hexagram 56: Traveler

52

To teach without words
and to increase without acting—
nothing in the world compares.

Daodejing 43

53

A great square has no corners,
a great vessel takes long to make,
a great sound is a faint tone,
a great image has no shape,

Tao is hidden without a name.
But only Tao has the perfection
to bring completion.

Daodejing 41

54

When old, we only want calm,
and we lose interest in all else.
I even lack plans to care for myself.
Empty of schemes, I return to old woods,
loosen my sash to pine breezes,
and play my qin in mountain moonlight.
You ask if failure passes to success?
Let a fishing song sound from shore to depths.

> "Reply to Vice Prefect Zhang," Wang Wei (699–759)

無名

55

Doing good takes repeated milling.

> Proverb

56

Heaven inside a mountain
is the image of great restraint.
A noble one frequently studies
words and deeds of the past
to raise their own virtue.

> *Yijing,* Image of hexagram 26: Great Restraint

57

Those who know do not speak.
Those who speak do not know.

Seal your mouth,
   block the doors,
   blunt your blades,
   untie your knots,
   temper the bright,
   settle with the dust.
This is called "uniting with Mystery."

Then you will be
beyond favor
   and beyond loss;
beyond profit
   and beyond harm;
beyond honor
   and beyond disgrace.

Yet you will be among the greatest in the world.

Daodejing 56

Nourish your breath-energy beyond words and rules.

Settle your heart, and act by not acting.

Still all movement, know the ancestral model.

Nothing truly matters—so who is it who searches?

True constancy must fit everything.

To fit everything requires no confusion.

The self abides in this unconfused nature.

When one's nature abides, breath-energy restores itself.

With the breath-energy restored, the dantian is firm.

In one pot mix Water and Fire.

Yin and yang are born, return, and renew.

The mundane is transformed in a single clap of thunder.

The pilgrim climbs to the white clouds in the head.

Sweet dew sprinkles Mount Meru.

Drink the wine of immortality for yourself.

Be at leisure—who needs to care?

Sit and listen—yet no string bends.

Understand through nature's works.

Everything comes through these twenty lines.

Climb them like heaven's ladder.

"The One Hundred Word Stela," Lu Dongbin (b. 796)

59

My words are easy to understand
and easy to practice.
But in all the world
no one understands
and no one practices.

My words have principle
and meaning
to make a system.

Daodejing 70

60

Empty your neck, raise your power to the crown.
Sink your breath-energy to the dantian.
Move evenly and do not lean.
Vanish suddenly, appear suddenly.

Shanxi Wang Zongyue's Taijiquan Treatise

61

True words are not beautiful.
Beautiful words are not true.

Daodejing 81

無
名

4 陰陽

Yin Yang

62

All things carry yin and embrace yang.
Coursing breath brings harmony.

Daodejing 42

63

On a high couch, we pass the time in the South Study;
the new moon rises through the open curtains.
Clear light streams through the woods onto fresh water
and it flows to our window in waves. Over time
how many periods of full and empty are there?
Yet so clearly the past changes to the present.
Beauties sing distinctly from the riverbank,
but at night in Yue, the songs must be bitter.
How can you be a thousand miles away?
Breezes blow away the scent of orchids.

"In the South Study with My Brother, Enjoying the Moon, and
Thinking of Vice Prefect Cui in Shanyin," Wang Changling
(698–765)

64

Sky and fire
give us the image of the kindred.
A noble one groups and sorts all things.

Yijing, Image of hexagram 13: Kindred

65

This is the month of the shortest day,
when yin and yang contend
and all of life pools.
A noble one distinguishes the signs.
They serve while protecting themselves
and make their desires serene.
They do away with sounds and colors,
restrict their wants,
and pacify their bodily drives.
They strive for stillness in all matters
and wait for yin and yang to settle.
The rue plant begins to sprout,
the lychee emerges,
earthworms curl,
elk shed their antlers,
the springs gush,
and the solstice arrives.
We chop trees and fine bamboo.

Book of Rites, "Seasons of the Months"

66

This is the month of the longest day,
when yin and yang contend
and death divides from life.
A noble one distinguishes the signs.
They serve while protecting themselves
and avoiding tension.
They avoid exciting sound and colors,
and do not strive.
They taste flavors sparingly,
without having to blend them.
They contain their desires
and settle the energy of their hearts.
The hundred officials are calm in all matters
and there are no punishments,
and so all is complete in calm and gentleness.
Deer shed their antlers.
Cicadas begin to buzz.
Mid-summer comes alive
and the hibiscus is glorious.

Book of Rites, "Seasons of the Months"

67

All the world knows beauty as beautiful—
    and so they know ugliness too.
Everyone knows goodness as good—
    and so they know bad too.

Daodejing 2

68

A wooden frame above water
is the image of a well.
A noble one works for the people
and urges union.

Yijing, Image of hexagram 48: Well

69

By the Jiang and Han, a homebound traveler broods.
Between heaven and earth: one wretched scholar.
A lone cloud: both the sky and I are far away.
A long night: the moon and I are both lonesome.
The setting sun: yet my heart is still ambitious.
The autumn wind: I can't recover from illness.
Since olden times: old horses were kept,
not necessarily chosen, for the sake of going far.

"The Jiang and Han River," Du Fu (712–770)

70

So nothing and everything are born together:
    difficulty and ease complete one another,
    long and short make one another,
    high and low come from one another,
    pitch and tone harmonize with each other,
    before and after follow one another.

    Daodejing 2

71

In the time of the sages,
they took heaven and earth as their certain basis.
They took yin and yang as the beginning and end,
the four seasons as the framework,
the sun and the stars as direction and pacing,
and the moon to set periods of time.
They included ghosts and spirits as followers,
the Five Phases as the basis for all matter,
ritual and conduct as their instrument,
human nature as their fields,
and the four mystical animals to cultivate.

    Book of Rites, "Applying Ritual"

72

Yin and yang must always be kept in mind.
To stick is to go.
To go is to stick.
Yang must never leave yin.
Yin must never leave yang.
Yin and yang multiply together.

Shanxi Wang Zongyue's Taijiquan Treatise

73

Night at Bull Island, West River.
Not a shred of cloud in the blue sky.
Boarding the boat, I glance at the autumn moon.
I remember General Xie, but it's in vain.
I might just as well sing out loud—
but no one is here to listen to my song.
Tomorrow I will hoist my sail and steer
where maple leaves swirl everywhere.

"Recalling the Past during a Night-Mooring at Bull Island,"
Li Bai (701–762)

74

Wind beneath the sky
is the image of mating.
A queen gives commands
to the four directions.

> *Yijing,* Image of hexagram 44: Copulating

75

Blunt the sharp,
untie the tangled,
temper the bright,
settle with the dust.

> *Daodejing* 4

76

That old saying that "the bent becomes whole"
    was no empty phrase!
All true wholeness goes back to that!

> *Daodejing* 22

77

The sun is new, the moon changes.

> Proverb

78

Time is light and dark, and like flowing water
it goes and never turns back.

Proverb

79

Great achievement viewed as imperfection
    is used without wrong.
Great fullness as a great channel
    is used without fail.

Great straightness seems crooked.
Great skill seems crude.
Great eloquence seems mumbled.

Movement overcomes cold,
stillness overcomes hot.
Pure stillness corrects all the world.

Daodejing 45

5

悲

Sorrow

Choked sobs follow when death parts us—
life's partings are ever sorrow on sorrow.
Jiangnan is a place filled with malaria
and no news arrived after your exile.

Then, old friend, you entered into my dreams,
as vividly as I remembered you.
The emperor's net holds you far away,
so how did you fly over here?

You, a soul trying to avoid blame all your life,
are now on a long road without any measure:
a soul arriving at a green maple forest,
a soul returning to a black mountain pass.

The moon dips and lights the roof beam in the house,
but it cannot illuminate your face.
How the waterway thrashes and its waves roil,
having lost its water dragon's control.

"Dreaming of Li Bai 1," Du Fu (712–770)

81

Water over fire
is the image of already-across.
A noble one thinks about suffering
and prepares to meet it.

Yijing, Image of hexagram 63: Already Across

82

We dismount to drink good wine,
and I ask where you will go.
You say, "I am discontented,
and will retire to Nanshan.
I'll go; no one will hear I've gone back:
a white cloud's time has no end."

"Farewell," Wang Wei (699–759)

83

Thunder over the mountain
is the image of a little excess.
A noble one always gives
a little more when acting,
never goes too far in grief,
and remains more than frugal.

Yijing, Image of hexagram 62: Small Crossing

84

A beautiful reputation is hard to get, but easy to lose.

> Proverb

85

This recluse returns to solitary rest,
slow thoughts cleansed by lonely purity.
I hold them, but I'd be glad if high-flying birds
would carry my emotions far away.
Day and night, I empty my heart of desire,
but don't those with feeling find the essence?
Whether to soar or drop, I stay in seclusion—
yet what comfort is there in my devotion?

> "Lament 3," Zhang Jiuling (673–740)

86

The nation is shattered, but mountains and rivers remain,
and the city walls will be sunken in grass by next spring.
Feeling the times, the flowers splash with tears.
Regretting our parting, birds cry with shock.
Warning beacons have blazed three months in a row.
A letter from home is worth ten thousand pieces of gold.
I scratch my white hair. It's too thin now—
so sparse that no hairpins will stay put.

> "Spring View," Du Fu (712–770)

87

The rites of mourning
are the utmost expression of sorrow and grief.
But sorrow must reach its limits
over the course of many events.
A noble person thinks of this from the start.

Book of Rites, "Tan Gong, II"

88

No water in the lake
is the image of distress.
A noble one stakes their life
on following their will.

Yijing, Image of hexagram 47: Distress

89

In Yan, the grass is like jade threads.
In Qin, green mulberry hangs low.
Should you ever yearn to come back,
I will be heartbroken by then.
The spring wind is no acquaintance;
why should it enter my gauze curtains?

"Spring Thoughts," Li Bai (701–762)

90

Heaven and earth parting
is the image of blockage.
A noble one acts with modest virtue
in the face of harsh hatred—
and when no way is open
to glory or joy.

Yijing, Image of hexagram 12: Clogging

悲

91

On my way back from battles abroad, I halt
my horse to say goodbye at your lonely grave.
Recent tears have left no dirt dry,
and broken clouds hang low in the sky.

You could have played chess with Tutor Xie.
Now I offer this sword, as if to Lord Xu.
As I leave, I see flowers dropping in the woods,
and hear weeping orioles sending me off.

"Leaving the Grave of Grand Marshall Fang," Du Fu (712–770)

92

Combined mountains
are the image of stillness.
A noble one doesn't think
beyond their lot.

悲

Yijing, Image of hexagram 52: Stillness

93

Sharp winds fill the towering sky. Apes howl sadly.
Birds circle the water to a white sand island.
Uncontained, the trees shed their leaves desolately down.
Endlessly, the Yangzi River froths, churns, and surges on.
Ten thousand miles of grief. Each autumn I'm always a
    sojourner.
One hundred years of illness:
    I must still take the stage alone.
Challenges, hardships, and regrets
    frost my temples still more.
My new disappointment:
    that I must quit the cloudy wine cup.

"Climbing High," Du Fu (712–770)

94

Tonight in Fuzhou, she sees
the moon alone in her room.
Far away, I pity our children
who don't know why we're apart,
or who don't remember Chang'an.
Her hair is damp with fragrant mist,
the clear light chills her jade arms.
When might we both lean at that window,
a pair in the light with dried tears?

"Moonlit Night," Du Fu (712–770)

95

At the gate, all the grass lies withered.
We're about to part and we're filled with grief.
The road abroad leads through cold and clouds—
no return until the season of snow and dusk.
Young and alone, you became a wanderer early.
You faced many hardships and advancement was slow.
Surprising tears, facing each other—empty.
Windblown travels ahead: will we meet again?

"Farewell to Li Duan," Lu Lun (739–799)

悲

96

The people of Tao who would advise a lord
won't try to conquer the world by great troops.

Such tactics rebound.
Briars and thorns spring up
wherever armies go.
    Sorrow follows behind a great host.

Good generals halt once they reach their goals.
    They don't dare risk more with their troops.

Win without pride.
Win without looting.
Win without swagger.
Win without brashness.
Win without cruelty.

When things grow big,
    they become old.
That goes against Tao.
What is against Tao
    dies young.

Daodejing 30

悲

6

求

Seeking

97

They say to find Chrysanthemum River,
go trace the waters of Green Creek,
follow ten thousand mountain turns
and a course of almost a hundred miles
splashing and crashing over riprap.
Deep calm color under the pines,
water chestnut and floating-heart ripple,
reeds reflect in limpid pools.
My heart remains plain and calm
and it's as pure as the river.
I only ask to stay on this flat rock
lingering with my fishing pole.

"Green Creek," Wang Wei (699–759)

98

Diligence brings abundance.

Proverb

99

Wind and thunder
give us the image of increase.
A noble one adjusts to the good they see,
and they correct their own mistakes.

Yijing, Image of hexagram 42: Increase

求

100

On North Mountain in white clouds,
you have happily secluded yourself.
Starting the long climb to see you,
my heart soars with the wild geese above.
I might worry since dusk is falling,
but the clear autumn air lifts me.
Late in the day I see villagers heading home
waiting for the ferry on the gravel shore.
Trees pack the horizon in clumps,
the riverbank curves like a crescent moon.
Could you meet me and bring wine?
We'll drink to the Double Nine Festival!

"Climbing Orchid Mountain in Autumn, Sent to Zhang Wu,"
Meng Haoran (689/691–740)

101

Water blocked by a mountain
is the image of obstacles.
A noble one turns inward
to cultivate virtue.

Yijing, Image of hexagram 39: Hindered

102

Pay attention to the waist area at every moment.
Keep the inside of your abdomen relaxed,
keep your breath-energy still, turn correctly.
Keep your tailbone centered, let your spirit penetrate to
    your crown.
Keep your entire body light, gain by holding your head up as
    if suspended.
Give great attention to the direction you face,
how you bend, how you stretch open, and how you close.
    Listen freely.

Shanxi Wang Zongyue's Taijiquan Treatise, "The Song of Practicing the Thirteen Dynamics"

103

The sun angles below the western mountain range;
valley after valley plunges abruptly into dark.
The moon rises through pines, the night grows cold;
I listen to the wind and the stream, full and pure.
The woodsmen trudge homeward, wanting rest;
birds search through cooking smoke for perches to settle.
You promised to come and stay for a time:
I'm alone with my qin at this vine-draped path.

> "At the Mountain House of My Teacher, Waiting in Vain for Elder
> Ding," Meng Haoran (689/691–740)

104

The look of heaven. The color of water.
West Lake is good.
Creatures in the clouds are fresh,
gulls and egrets sleep idly.
I follow my routine, listening to pipes and strings.

Wind. Clear moon, slanting white, a perfect night.
One piece of jade field.
Who needs a horse or phoenix?
One person on a boat is an immortal.

> "The Look of Heaven, the Color of Water," Ouyang Xiu
> (1007–1072)

105

Among the ten thousand things,
Tao is the most profound.
It is the treasure of good people
and the protector of bad people.

Beautiful words are sold at the market.
Noble deeds can be presented as a gift.
But even bad people are not abandoned.

A king is enthroned as the son of heaven
and appoints his three ministers.
The nobles may present their jade disks
and parade their teams of horses,
but it's not as good as presenting Tao.

Why did the ancients prize Tao so much?
Was it not because
it could be had by any who sought it,
and that the guilty could find forgiveness in it?
That is why it is the treasure of the world.

Daodejing 62

106

Farmers hoe the grain, even at noon.
Sweat drips onto the grain, then the earth.
Who thinks of this over a plate of food—
that each grain comes from so much toil?

"Sympathy for the Farmers," Li Shen (d. 846)

107

The master brings you to the gate:
self-cultivation depends on you.

Proverb

108

To enter the gate and to be guided on the route,
you must have verbal instruction,
but putting the principles into use
without violating the teachings
requires your own constant effort.

Shanxi Wang Zongyue's Taijiquan Treatise, "The Song of Practicing the Thirteen Dynamics"

109

Thunder in the center of the earth
is the image of returning.
The ancient kings closed the borders
at the solstice so that merchants did not travel
and kings did not tour the provinces.

Yijing, Image of hexagram 24: Returning

110

This is the road where rebels forced our surrender
when they overran the outskirts from the west.
I've lived in terror since then, even to this day,
and I haven't yet recaptured my soul.
We have just regained the capital city;
already I'm sent abroad and must obey.
I lack talent, and grow older each day:
I stop my horse to gaze at the thousand gates.

"Huazhou," Du Fu (712–770)

111

Without passing through each effort
one cannot increase one's wisdom.

Proverb

112

Garrison drums cut off people's travels
along the frontier in autumn. A lone goose calls.
After tonight, the dew will turn to frost.
How bright the moon seemed in my hometown.
Although I have brothers, we're all scattered,
with no family left to ask if we're alive or dead.
Letters take too long and may not arrive.
This is how it is: war without end.

"Remembering My Brothers on a Moonlit Night,"
Du Fu (712–770)

113

The bright moon rises above the sea;
the world should be joined in this moment.
How this lover laments the growing night—
my yearning builds as evening comes.

Snuff the candle, spare its brightness,
wear a sleeping robe as the dew grows.
I can't bear what I want to give you:
I lie down to dream of being together.

"Gazing at the Moon and Thinking of You Far Away," Zhang
Jiuling (673–740)

114

Rolling thunder
is the image of shaking.
A noble one searches
their own morals
with fear and dread.

Yijing, Image of hexagram 51: Thunder

求

115

People go hungry
when officials eat too much in taxes.
Hungry people
are hard to govern
when officials overly burden them.

People take death lightly
when it's too awful to seek life.
When people take death lightly,
it means we should let them live—
and value precious life.

Daodejing 75

7

週
迴

Cycles

116

Reversal is the movement of Tao.
　　Yielding is the usage of Tao.

All the creatures of the world
　　were born from being.

All existence was born
　　from nonbeing.

Daodejing 40

117

Returning is its Tao.

Yijing, Statement of hexagram 24: Returning

118

Heaven's movement is constant.
It is not for Yao to keep.
It is not for Jie to lose.

> *Xunzi*, "Heavenly Treatise"

週
迴

119

Black clouds fly: their ink does not hide the hills.
White rain leaps, drops pell-mell into the boats.
Wind sweeps the earth, suddenly blows it all away.
I see the lake below: the water is like the sky.

> "Written While Drunk in Lake-View Pavilion on
> the Twenty-Seventh Day of the Sixth Month," Su Shi (1037–1101)

120

Thunder and rain
are the image of release.
A noble one forgives mistakes
and pardons wrongs.

> *Yijing*, Image of hexagram 40: Releasing

121

A high guest house with the traveler gone.
A small garden where petals fly in confusion.
They fall in zig-zags along a crooked path
and they stretch as far as the setting sun.
Wrenched inside, I can't bear to sweep.
Eyes downcast, I wish that they could last.
A tender heart is spent by the end of spring—
and all that's gained is a tear-soaked robe.

"Falling Petals," Li Shangyin (813?–858?)

122

There was something nebulous
before heaven and earth were born.
    Still! Empty!
    Standing alone without change,
    revolving without cease—
it may be called the Mother of the World.
I do not know its name.
    The word I give it is "Tao."
    If pressed, I call it "great."

Daodejing 25

123

I petition no more at the north gate
and return to a shabby hut on South Mountain.
Untalented, the enlightened ruler banished me.
My illnesses are many, my friends are few.
White hair seems to rush my aging.
Each new spring wears the years away.
Worries always in mind, I can't sleep.
Moonlit pines; night window; ruins.

"Returning at Year's End to South Mountain," Meng Haoran
(689/691–740)

124

Falling leaves return to the roots.

Proverb

125

Great, it reaches out.
Reaching out, it goes far.
Going far, it returns.

Daodejing 25

126

Mountain light falls suddenly in the west.
Moon in the east rises slowly over a lake.
I loosen my hair to enjoy the cool night,
lie relaxed at the open pavilion window.
Fragrance of lotus drifts on the breeze,
pure dewdrops patter from lotus leaves.
I want to fetch my qin and play it,
but I'm sorry no friend is here to listen.
Such feelings as I think of you, old friend:
companion only in my midnight dreams!

"Summertime at South Pavilion, Missing Elder Xin,"
Meng Haoran (689/691–740)

127

The sun sets and the moon rises.
The moon sets and the sun rises.

Sun and moon alternate with each other,
and so brightness results.

The cold goes and the heat comes.
The heat goes and the cold comes.

Cold and heat alternate with each other
and so a year is completed.

Yijing, The Great Treatise II

128

Ancestors plant trees;
descendants enjoy cool shade.

> Proverb

129

Wild geese fly south in the tenth month.
I hear this is where they turn around.
But I'm unable to leave here.
When will I ever get back home?

The river is still. The tide will turn.
The forests are smothered in noxious air.
I'll look tomorrow toward my native home,
and imagine I see the Gansu plum trees.

> "Inscribed at a Relay Station North of the Dayu Mountains,"
> Song Zhiwen (656?–712?)

130

A thousand hills, but no birds fly.
Ten thousand paths, without anyone's tracks.
A lonely boat, a big straw hat, an old man
fishing alone in the cold river snow.

> "River Snow," Liu Zongyuan (773–819)

131

All my life, I have loved the good West Lake.
Crowds gather around the red wheels,
riches and honor float like clouds,
glance down and up and twenty springs have passed.
Now that I've returned, I look like a crane from the distant
    east.
The people at the city wall—
every one I see is new.
Who will recognize their old governor?

> "All My Life I Have Loved It (Picking Mulberries),"
> Ouyang Xiu (1007–1072)

週
廻

132

At the end of the day, heaven's power warms and dries.
Its Tao is to turn and return.

> *Yijing,* Hexagram 1: Heaven

Tao

133

The great Tao flows everywhere!
It can go left and right.
All things rely on it for life; it does not deny them.
When its work is done, it doesn't claim credit.
It clothes and feeds all beings with no demand to be their
    lord.
It wants nothing from them.

You might call it small,
yet all things return to it
without anyone's direction.

You could call it great.
Since it claims no greatness for itself
in the end, its greatness is complete.

Daodejing 34

134

In middle-age, I found the right Tao.
and I made my home at South Mountain.
I rise and wander the land in beautiful solitude.
Problems overcome, I know the empty self.
I walk and reach the point where the stream begins,
sit and watch for the moment when clouds rise,
sometimes I happen to meet an old woodsman.
We talk and laugh, with no hurry to go.

"Retreat to Zhongnan Mountains," Wang Wei (699–759)

135

Fire above, a lake below,
is the image of estrangement.
A noble one keeps with those who are the same
yet allows for those who are different.

Yijing, Image of hexagram 38: Estrangement

136

At the end of the day, heaven's power warms and dries.
Its Tao is to turn and return.

Yijing, Hexagram 1: Heaven

137

Draw well water; the cold shakes my teeth.
I clear my heart, brush the dust from my robes,
and solemnly lift a palm-leaf book.
I recite with each step to the east study hall.
I have not yet found the root of the truth,
overlooked it as I pursued this life's path.
How I aspire to these deep and sagely words
hoping that I can cultivate my nature in full.
I find the hall of the Way quiet and still,
amid colorful moss and dark bamboo.
Sun glimmers in the mist and heavy dew.
Pines appear bathed in the thickest paste.
Tranquil, suddenly I leave both words and speech:
Awareness! Joy! My heart is finally content.

> "Visiting Master Chao's Temple at Daybreak to Read a Zen
> Scripture," Liu Zongyuan (773–819)

道

138

Heaven's Tao is change and transformation.
All things are ordered, all characters are certain.
With all protected and united, there is great harmony
and in this all is beneficial and pure.
It leads to all the various things
and sets the myriad nations in repose.

> *Yijing*, Hexagram 1: Heaven

139

Brightness above the earth
is the image of advancing.
A noble one uses
their own brilliance
to highlight virtue.

Yijing, Image of hexagram 35: Advancing

140

Sitting alone in dense bamboo,
plucking my qin and singing along.
No one knows that I'm deep in the woods.
Bright moon comes: together we shine.

"The Bamboo Retreat," Wang Wei (699–759)

141

Tranquil!
    As it will always be!
I don't know whose child it is,
    but it was here before any gods.

Daodejing 4

142

Heaven's Tao sends down relief
　　and so is brilliant and bright.
Earth's Tao is low
　　and yet it travels upward.
Heaven's Tao diminishes the full
　　and yet benefits humble people.
Earth's Tao transforms the full
　　and so circulates humble people.
Ghosts and spirits injure the full
　　and so bless the humble people.
The human way is to shun the full
　　and value the humble.

Humble, respectful, yet brilliant.
Lowly, yet without excess:
the summation of the noble one.

Yijing, Hexagram 15: Humility

143

Strategy: it's a nation's great task,
the basis of life and death,
the Tao of survival or destruction:
it can never be ignored.

Sunzi's Art of Strategy, "Laying Plans"

144

On the route past blue mountains,
our boat glides along green waters.
Currents spread wide to both banks,
wind quickly fills our open sail.
The rising sun dispels the night.
Spring on the river turns age back.
How can I send letters home?
With the wild geese who pass Luoyang.

"Beneath Beigu Mountain," Wang Wan (693–751)

145

When the great Tao is no longer followed,
    then benevolence and justice arise.
When knowledge and intelligence appear,
    then great hypocrisy occurs.
When the six relations are no longer at peace,
    then filial piety and charity emerge.
When nation and clans grow corrupt,
    then loyal ministers arrive.

Daodejing 18

146

Returning alone to the middle path:
that's how to follow Tao.

Yijing, Hexagram 24: Returning

147

Bright—but not by rising.
Dim—but not by sinking.
Relentless—but can't be named.
Returns repeatedly—but has no substance.

Call it formless form
   or image of nothing.
Call it fleeting and indistinct.
   You can meet it yet not see its head.
   You can follow it yet not see its back.

Daodejing 14

148

Where is heaven's highway?
There is Tao's great movement.

Yijing, Hexagram 26: Great Restraint

149

The sun sets westward behind Yan.
I call at the thatched hut of a single monk.
Only fallen leaves—where could he be?
In cold clouds? On a road of many levels?
Alone, he strikes the stone bell each evening,
and might then lean idly on his rattan staff.
    This world is but a tiny grain of dust.
    I should pacify all my loves and hates.

"North Green Vines," Li Shangyin (813?–858?)

150

Keep the great image
    and the world follows.
Go without hurting
    and great peace follows.
Music and delicacies
    will entice passing guests.

When Tao emerges,
    it seems weak and without flavor.
It's seen, but indistinct.
    Heard, but barely audible.
Still it can be used without end.

Daodejing 35

151

Great virtue
follows only from Tao.

What we call Tao
is elusive and obscure.
Sudden! Faint!
    Yet forms come from its core.
Dim! Abrupt!
    Yet beings come from its core.
Obscure! Dark!
    Yet life-force comes from its core.

That life-force is quite true,
and its core has been trusted
from ancient times until now,
and the named things
have never ceased to come from it.

Through it, we can see the Father of Everything.
How do I know it is the Father of Everything?
By all of the above!

Daodejing 21

There are five factors
when officers are planning
and searching their feelings:

道

First is Tao.
Second is heaven.
Third is earth.
Fourth is the general.
Fifth is method.

Tao means that the people will accord with a ruler's will.
Whether it's death or whether it's life, they will fear no
danger.
Heaven means yin and yang, cold and hot, the season and
time.
Earth means far and near, difficult or easy conditions, wide
or narrow terrain, and the possibilities of death and life.
The general must be wise, trustworthy, humane,
courageous, and strict.
Method means proper order, disciplined officers, and to be
of use to the sovereign.

Every general knows these five factors.
Those who know will win.
Those who don't know will lose.

Sunzi's Art of Strategy, "Laying Plans"

153

All the world says that my Tao is great,
even if it doesn't look that way.
But it's great because it has no appearance.
It would look petty if it had an appearance!

Daodejing 67

154

Heaven's Tao is like pulling a bow—
what is high is pulled low,
what is low is pulled high.
    Heaven's Tao
    is to lessen what is too much
    and add to what is too little.

But that is not the Tao of people—
they take from the poor
to add to their own.
    Who will take their own wealth
    and serve others?
    Only one who has Tao!

Therefore the wise act but claim not credit,
make achievements without dwelling on them,
and make no display of their worth.

Daodejing 77

155

When superior scholars hear of Tao,
    they practice it diligently.
When mediocre scholars hear of Tao,
    they grasp for it but lose it.
When inferior scholars hear of Tao,
    they laugh at it.

If they didn't laugh enough, it wouldn't be Tao.

Thus the writers hold:
    The bright Tao seems dim,
    the advancing Tao seems to retreat,
    the straight Tao seems knotted,
    superior virtue seems like loss,
    great purity seems humble,
    vast virtue seems insufficient,
    found virtue seems lost,
    solid truth seems to waver.

Daodejing 41

9 天地 Heaven and Earth

156

Heaven is eternal, earth lasts long.
The reason why heaven and earth
are eternal and last long
is because they do not live for themselves.
That's why they endure forever.

Daodejing 7

157

Heaven and earth are everywhere.
and richly transform the ten thousand things.
The essence of male and female intermingles
and transforms and births the ten thousand things.

Yijing, The Great Treatise II

158

Fortunate is the person whose self is in accord with heaven.

Proverb

159

I have long heard of Dongting Lake.
Now I climb Yueyang Gate Tower
dividing Wu and Chu to the south and east.
Here floats heaven and earth, day and night.
Not one word arrives from family or friends.
Old and sick, all I have is a lonely boat.
War horses block the mountains in the north.
I lean on the pavilion rail, weeping and sobbing.

"Climbing Yueyang Gate Tower," Du Fu (712–770)

160

Heaven moving
is the image of vigor.
A noble one strengthens
themselves without pause.

Yijing, Image of hexagram 1: Heaven

161

In front, no one sees those of the past.
Behind, no one sees those yet to come.
We ponder how heaven and earth last and last:
alone and sad, we can't stop the tears that fall.

"Song of Climbing the Youzhou Terrace," Chen Zi'ang
(661?–702)

162

Sparse grass, a light wind along the shore,
the tall mast of my lone boat in the night.
Stars hang over the broad, flat plain.
The moon rushes along the great river current.
How could I ever make a name by writing?
Old and sick, I should rest from my duties.
Floating, fluttering, what am I?
A single gull between heaven and earth.

"Thoughts Written While Traveling at Night," Du Fu (712–770)

163

Fire in the center of a lake
is the image of reform.
A noble one sets their timing
clearly by the seasons.

Yijing, Image of hexagram 49: Reform

164

Heaven and earth change and transform
grass, trees, and all things.

Yijing, hexagram 2: Earth

165

Heaven and earth joined
is the image of prospering.
Be like the queen who
granted wealth, fulfilled
the Tao of heaven and earth,
and helped fit people on all sides
to both heaven and earth.

Yijing, Image of hexagram 11: Prospering

166

Away, away: the basic way of grass.
Each year, the withered becomes green again.
Wildfire can never seem to burn it all:
it comes to life again in the spring wind.
How that scent pervades the ancient road,
clear skies, jade green up to the city ruins.
Again I say goodbye to my honored friend:
emotions are abundant and full as we part.

"Poem of Farewell on the Basic Cause of Grass," Bai Juyi
(772–846)

Since my youth, what was popular didn't suit me;
my basic character was love of hills and mountains.
Mistakenly, I fell into the dusty net,
and trapped, I lost all of thirty years.
A caged bird yearns for the ancient forest;
a fish kept in a pond will miss old waters.
I'll clear the wasteland at the southern border,
I'll stay honest and pure, and keep to the fields.
Around my house, I have more than ten acres,
and my thatched hut has eight or nine spans.
Elms and willows shade my back eaves;
peach and plum are heaped in the front hall.
The nearest hamlet is dim in the distance;
its smoke seems reluctant to leave the village.
Dogs bark from deep within the lanes;
chickens squawk through the tops of mulberry trees.
No dust swirls through my courtyard door;
empty rooms offer abundant leisure.
For so long, I felt that I lived in a prison.
I'm restored, content to return to nature.

"Returning to Live on the Farm, 1," Tao Yuanming (365–427)

168

Fire in the sky above
is the image of great holdings.
A noble one curbs the bad,
spreads the good,
and serves the will of heaven.

Yijing, Image of hexagram 14: Great Holdings

169

The Son of Heaven sacrificed to heaven and earth.
Rulers of the vassal states sacrificed to the gods of the soil
    and grain.
Great men offered the Five Sacrifices.

The Son of Heaven sacrificed to heaven,
and then to the famous mountains and great rivers.

The Five Sacred Peaks were as honored as the Three Great
    Ministers.
The Four Rivers were seen as honored as the rulers of the
    states.
The princes sacrificed to the famous mountains and great
    rivers in their own lands.

Book of Rites, "Summary of the Rules of Propriety, Part 2"

Humans rise from the virtuous power of heaven and earth,
the combination of yin and yang,
the interaction of ghosts and spirits,
and the subtle energy of the Five Phases.
From the start, heaven controlled yang
and hung the sun and stars.
Earth controlled yin
and gave channel to the mountains and streams.

The Five Phases spread throughout the four seasons.
When they reached harmony, the moon was produced,
and that is why it waxes for fifteen days
and wanes for fifteen days
in alternations of great effort and exhaustion.

The Five Phases, the four seasons, the twelve months—
each one comes to prominence.
The five notes, the six fundamentals, the twelve pitch-pipes—
each one can be the tonic tone.
The five flavors, the six condiments, the twelve foods—
each one has its substance.
The five colors, the six figures, the twelve kinds of clothes—
each one has its place and use.
So people are the heart of heaven and earth
and part of the Five Phases, born of food, flavors,
distinctions, sound, and color.

Book of Rites, "The Use of Ceremony"

171

Heaven and earth combine,
and afterward all things arise.
Thus, marriage is the beginning
of the ten thousand generations.

Book of Rites, "Jiao Te Sheng"

天地

172

Thus when the sages made the rules,
they took heaven and earth as their basis,
yin and yang as commencement,
the four seasons as authoritative,
the sun and stars to set the time,
the moon to set periods,
followed the ghosts and spirits,
understood substance by the Five Phases,
made rites and righteousness as their instrument,
the character of people as their fields,
and the four creatures for domestication.

Book of Rites, "The Use of Ceremony"

173

The great person

follows heaven and earth
　　and joins with their virtue,
follows the sun and moon,
　　and joins with their brightness,
follows the four seasons
　　and joins with their sequence,
follows the ghosts and spirits
　　and joins with their good and bad influences.

They may act before heaven,
　　but heaven will be with them.
They may act after heaven,
　　yet they respect heaven's season.

　　　　Yijing, hexagram 1: Heaven

10

Mystery

玄

174

Be without desires to see the original constant
    and glimpse the subtle.
Constant hankering
    only lets you see outlines.

These two are really the same—
    they simply have two names.
Together, we call them profound.
Deeply profound, they are the openings to all mystery.

Daodejing 1

175

All is born, grows, and lives
without being owned.
All thrives without meddling.
All moves without any directors.
That is called Mysterious Virtue.

Daodejing 10

176

Deep doubts, deep wisdom;
little doubt, little wisdom.

> Proverb

玄

177

Ten years apart with the world in unrest.
We meet again—you've grown into a man.
When we met, I had to ask your family name.
Hearing it, I remembered your youthful self.
This world changes like the vast ocean.
We don't stop talking until the evening bell.
Tomorrow you travel the Baling Road,
the autumns and mountains heavy between us.

> "Happily Seeing My Cousin Again Only to Talk of Parting
> Again," Li Yi (748?–827?)

178

Light plunging into the earth
is the image of smothered brightness.
A noble one governs the masses
by being indirect yet clear.

> *Yijing*, Image of hexagram 36: Smothered Light

179

Beyond Taiyi Peak near our heavenly capital,
mountains extend to the edge of the sea.
White clouds converge as I look back:
blue vapor engulfs all in sight.
Cleaving space, the mountains alter all;
cloudy or clear, every valley differs.
Needing shelter, some place to spend the night.
I call to a woodcutter across the water.

"Zhongnan (Taiyi) Mountains," Wang Wei (699–759)

180

Life and nonbeing,
action and failure,
eternity and disorder—
together they are called
Mysterious Virtue.

Daodejing 51

玄

181

Who knows of Massed Fragrance Temple,
on a peak countless miles in the clouds
through ancient woods where no one passes,
    but where a bell rings deep in the mountains?
Gushing of a spring through steep rock,
pale sun chilling the green pine trees.
Twilight emptiness mirrored on a pool:
    deep meditation curbs the poison dragon.

"Crossing to Massed Fragrance Temple," Wang Wei (699–759)

182

If you constantly know this standard,
then that's called Mysterious Virtue.

It is deep and wide, and helps
all creatures return to their natures
and reach the great accord.

Daodejing 65

11 Soft

183

The softest in the world
overcomes what is hardest.

Daodejing 43

184

The sky above and the lake below
give us the image of treading.
A noble one sorts high from low
and soothes the people's will.

Yijing, Image of hexagram 10: Walking

185

The water is soft. It's hard to know what to pursue.
The clouds come out. I don't want to go back again.
Melancholy spring wind, pained at river sunset.
This mandarin duck is alone—never with a flock.

"Farewell," Yu Xuanji (844–869)

186

When others are hard, I am soft;
that's called going.
When I follow, then others are hampered;
that's called sticking.

When others attack quickly, I respond quickly.
When others move slowly, I follow at leisure.
Although ten thousand variations may occur,
there is only one principle from start to finish.

Once this is familiar, you will slowly realize a strong
    understanding.
Once you realize a strong understanding, you will reach
    marvelous levels.
But unless you avoid using physical strength over a long
    period of time,
you will never have the flash of enlightenment that ties it all
    together.

Shanxi Wang Zongyue's Taijiquan Treatise

187

Put the strong and big below,
put the soft and weak above.

Daodejing 76

188

The valley spirit never dies.
Call it "Mysterious Female,"
or a gate, the root
of heaven and earth.
It remains softer than soft
and serves you with ease.

Daodejing 6

189

If you want to reduce,
  you should first expand.
If you want to weaken,
  you should first strengthen.
If you want to topple,
  you should first raise high.
If you want to remove,
  then first give.

This is called "reducing the bright."
The soft overcomes the hard
and the weak overcomes the strong.

Daodejing 36

190

A feather cannot be added.
A fly cannot land.
Others cannot know me,
but I alone know others.
A hero is unrivaled
because all possibilities have been covered.

Shanxi Wang Zongyue's Taijiquan Treatise

柔

191

At birth, we are soft and weak.
At death, we are hard and strong.
All things are this way.
Young grass and trees are soft and weak,
and at death are hard and strong.
Death follows the hard and strong.
Life follows the soft and weak.

Daodejing 76

192

A bully is always a coward.

Proverb

193

Thunder and lightning
are the image of biting and cracking.
The ancient kings made fines clear
and decreed the laws.

Yijing, Image of hexagram 21: Biting and Cracking

194

There are many approaches and systems.
Although powerful and with different techniques,
they generally don't go beyond the powerful bullying the
  weak
and the slow losing to the fast.
The strong beating the weak
and the slow hand losing to the swift hand
are a matter of innate ability
and have nothing to do with what can be learned.

Shanxi Wang Zongyue's Taijiquan Treatise

195

Tao is absolute but has no name.

Although it is simple and subtle,
no one has yet governed with it.
If rulers could hold to it,
everyone would yield to them.

Daodejing 32

196

Nothing in the world is softer and weaker than water,
yet for attacking the hard and strong, nothing is better.

Anything in the world can be changed.
Everyone knows that soft overcomes hard
and that weak overcomes strong,
but who can practice that?

Therefore, the wise say
one who takes on a nation's filth
becomes lord of fields and grain.
One who bears a nation's woes
becomes this world's ruler.
Right words seem odd.

Daodejing 78

197

Earth is the origin, our very basis,
amply birthing ten thousand things.
It submissively meets heaven.

柔

Earth greatly supports everything.
Its complete power is unlimited.
What it holds is immense; its brilliance is huge.
It conducts each thing and creature completely and
    smoothly.

The mare is a creature of the earth.
It gallops the earth without boundaries.
It is mild and submissive, good and pure.

The noble ones travel far.
If they take the initiative, they lose their Tao.
If they follow and submit, they find constancy.

Yijing, Hexagram 2: Earth

198

A three thousand meter dike can break
because of one ant's hole.

Proverb

199

Earth is very soft, but in moving it is hard and strong.
It is most still, yet its virtue is direct.
By following, it gains control, and yet it is constant.
It holds the ten thousand things, and yet its changes are
    brilliant.
Earth's Tao is to be submissive:
it receives heaven throughout the changing seasons.

> *Yijing*, Hexagram 2: Earth

柔

200

Fire is beautiful.
The sun and moon are beautiful in the sky.
Hundreds of grains, grasses, and trees are beautiful on the
    earth.
Great brightness is also beautiful and right.
There is change, and all under heaven is complete.
Soft beauty is central and correct
and thus all goes smoothly.
Nourish being as docile as a cow.

> *Yijing*, Hexagram 30: Fire

201

A noble one knows
what's nascent and knows what's manifest,
knows the soft and knows the hard,
and so ten thousand people look to them.

Yijing, The Great Treatise II

柔

202

Can you carry yourself
with your mind and soul as one
and not let them separate?

Can you keep your breath whole and soft
and become like a newborn child?

Can you cleanse your mystic vision
and become flawless?

Can you act without intellect
to love the people and rule the state?

Can you be gentle
in opening and closing
heaven's gate?

Can you reach an understanding
in all directions without "knowledge"?

Daodejing 10

12 善 Excellence

203

The greatest good is to be like water.
The good of water is that it benefits
all things without conflict.
It flows in places that people despise,
and so is akin to Tao.

Daodejing 8

204

Mountain bell rings of day's fading light.
Fisher folk clamor to board the ferry.
Others trudge the sandy river shore home.
I also board a boat, back to Deer Gate.
The moon shines through Deer Gate's misty trees.
Suddenly I reach Pang Gong's hermitage—
cliff-side gate, long still trail in pines.
Only a recluse can freely come and go.

"Song of a Night of Returning to Lumen Mountain,"
Meng Haoran (689/691–740)

205

Excellence not accumulated
    will not be enough to complete one's name.
Harms not accumulated
    will not be enough to destroy oneself.
Small people believe that even small excellences
    offer no gain, and so they don't try to achieve them.
They think that small harms are no threat
    and so they don't try to be rid of them.
Thus the harms accumulate until they cannot be covered,
    and when evil becomes great, it cannot be corrected.

Yijing, Great Treatise II

206

Clouds and thunder
are the image of sprouting.
A noble one can trace
the secret threads.

Yijing, Image of hexagram 3: Sprouting

207

An excellent beginning
puts effort closer to success.

Proverb

208

A good dwelling comes from the earth,
a good mind comes from depth,
a good ally comes from kindness,
a good word comes from trust,
a good government comes from rule,
a good outcome comes from ability,
a good movement comes from timing.

Daodejing 8

209

The white sun sets behind the peaks
and the Yellow River flows into the sea.
For a view of a thousand miles,
climb up to another level.

"Guanque Tower," Wang Zhihuan (688–742)

210

A mountain in the middle of the earth
is the image of humility.
A noble one amasses the many,
increases the small,
and balances things fairly.

Yijing, Image of hexagram 15: Humility

211

One who has such goodness does not fight
and is therefore free of fault.

Daodejing 8

212

A lake flooding the trees
is the image of great excess.
A noble one can stand alone without fear
and can renounce the world
without regrets.

Yijing, Image of hexagram 28: Great Excess

213

Some act without knowing why.
I don't do that.
I listen a great deal,
pick what's excellent,
and then I follow it.
I see much and comprehend.
This is the sequence of knowledge.

Analects, "Shu Er"

214

Holding anything to the utmost
    won't be as good as stopping short.
Tempering a blade to its sharpest
    won't keep it keen for long.
Filling a hall with gold and jade
    won't give you safety.
Prizing wealth and honor
    will invite blame on yourself.

After merit and success are reached,
    heaven's way is to withdraw.

   Daodejing 9

215

Wood growing on the mountain
is the image of gradualness.
A noble one keeps good virtue
and improves social customs.

   Yijing, Image of hexagram 53: Gradually

216

Every book holds a house of gold.

   Proverb

217

Don't try to be lustrous
    as precious jade.
Choose instead to be
    a string of common stones.

Daodejing 39

218

Fire at the foot of the mountain
is the image of forging ahead.
A noble one clarifies the many ways of governing
yet never dares to impede trials.

Yijing, Image of hexagram 22: Forging Ahead

219

We often fail because we ignore the close to search for the
    far.
Thus it's said: "Miss by a hair's breadth, err by a thousand
    miles."
To learn this means to distinguish all clearly;
that is why this treatise has been written.

Shanxi Wang Zongyue's Taijiquan Treatise

220

Learning is like rowing a boat against the current:
once you stop rowing,
    you drift backward.

    Proverb

221

Fame or yourself—
    which do you value more?
Yourself or your things—
    which is worth more?
What you have or what you might not get—
    which brings more worry?
So we see that great love leads to great loss,
    and great hoarding leads to certain ruin.

    Daodejing 44

222

If the excellent were to lead for one hundred years,
they could conquer oppression
and remove corruption.

    Analects, "Zi Lu"

What is well planted cannot be uprooted.
What is held tight cannot be removed.
Children and grandchildren
    should worship piously without end.

Cultivate yourself within.
    Make your virtue true.
Cultivate your family
    and virtue will overflow.
Cultivate your community
    and virtue will last long.
Cultivate your nation
    and virtue will be abundant.
Cultivate the world
    and virtue will be universal.

Therefore, when it comes
    to knowing the self, observe the self;
    to knowing the family, observe the family;
    to knowing the community, observe the community;
    to knowing the nation, observe the nation;
    to knowing the world, observe the world.

How do I know how the world is? By all this!

Daodejing 54

224

Approach people with respect.
Be filial, kind, and loyal.
Advance the excellent and teach those
who are not yet capable.

Analects, "Wei Zheng"

225

Sincere, true, excellent in learning,
committed until death, excellent in Tao.

They won't endanger the country.
They won't live in a chaotic state.

When all under heaven is with Tao,
they will be visible.
When there is no Tao, they remain hidden.

When a nation has Tao,
    poverty and lowliness are shameful.
When a nation has no Tao,
    abundance and wealth are shameful.

Analects, "Tai Bo"

226

Any worker who wishes to do well
must first sharpen their tools.

Analects, "Wei Ling Gong"

227

Three kinds of friends are beneficial:
upright friends,
tolerant friends,
and highly knowledgeable friends.
These are beneficial.
Friends who care for expedience,
friends whose excellence is weak,
and friends who glibly flatter
will bring injury.

Analects, "Ji Shi"

228

My excellence is in nourishing
my vast and abundant breath-energy.

Mengzi, "Gong Sun Chou I"

The excellent scholar of one village
will make friends with all the other
excellent scholars of that village.

The excellent scholar of one nation
will make friends with all the other
excellent scholars of that nation.

The excellent scholar of the world
will make friends with all the other
excellent scholars of the world.

When it's not enough to be friends
with the excellent scholars of the world,
then one turns to the ancients with esteem.

One lauds their poetry,
one studies their books,
and if one doesn't know of them as people,
then one studies their histories.
One becomes friends with the ancients.

Mengzi, "Wan Zhang II"

230

The excellent learner:
> even if the teacher's attention is elsewhere
> will achieve many times what another will
> and will only say that they are ordinary.

The poor learner:
> Even if the teacher is attentive
> will achieve only half of what another will
> and will only express resentment.

Book of Rites, "Xue Ji"

231

An excellent questioner
is like someone chopping a hard tree.
First, they deal with the easy,
then they deal with sections.
After a long time
in mutual discussion,
all is explained.

A poor questioner does the opposite.

Book of Rites, "Xue Ji"

232

The excellent teacher waits to be questioned.
It's like striking a bell.

Strike a bell lightly, and there will be little sound.
Strike a bell firmly, and there will be a big sound.
Strike it in succession, and what will follow is all its sound.

The poor teacher is the opposite.

This is how everyone should advance the Tao of learning.

Book of Rites, "Xue Ji"

233

When Shun lived deep in the middle of the mountains,
dwelling with trees and rock
and traveling with deer and boar,
how much did he as a mountain dweller
differ from someone in the fields?

Once he heard an excellent word
or saw a single excellent action,
he was like a bursting river,
abundant and irresistible.

Mengzi, "Jin Xin I"

234

For an excellent heart,
there is no greater excellence
than to reduce one's desires.

Mengzi, "Jin Xin II"

235

When one reaches Tao sincerely,
foreknowledge is possible:

When a nation or family is to rise,
surely there will be lucky omens.

When nation and family are about to perish,
surely there will be unlucky omens.

This can be seen through yarrow stalk
or tortoise shell, and they affect
the movement of the four limbs.

Whether misfortune or fortune,
the excellent know in advance.

Those who are not excellent
also know in advance.

Therefore, the sincere are like spirits.

Book of Rites, "Zhong Yu"

236

Words that seem close but point to something far away
are excellent words.
Guarding agreements while giving broadly
is the excellent Tao.
The words of the noble one
don't go outside the zone
and yet Tao remains.
When the noble one is observant
and cultivated, then there is peace under heaven.
The ongoing disease of people is this:
they neglect their own fields to pull the weeds of another.
What they ask of others is great,
but what they ask of themselves is small.

Mengzi, "Jin Kin II"

237

Ascribe good to others
and wrong to oneself
and the people will not fight.

Ascribe good to others
and wrong to oneself
and hatred and resentment will vanish.

Book of Rites, "Fang Ji"

238

When the scholars hear excellence,
they openly tell of it.
When they see excellence,
they openly reveal it.

When it comes to rank and position,
they let others go first.
When it comes to suffering and difficulties,
they will share in it until death.

No matter how long it's been,
they still wait patiently to help.
No matter how far it is,
they will still reach there.

That's how reliable and commendable they are.

Book of Rites, "Ru Xing"

239

A lake rising to meet the sky
is the image of certainty.
A noble one gives wealth to those below
and fears dwelling on their own merits.

Yijing, Image of hexagram 43: Decisiveness

240

The rivers and seas are lords
of one hundred streams
because they excel at being lowest.
That is why they are lords of all streams.

So if a sage intends to be above others,
    then a sage must be below them.
If a sage wishes to lead them,
    then a sage must be behind them.

In this way, even if the sage is above,
    people feel no weight.
If the sage leads, people fear no harm.

Therefore, everyone will joyously lend support
    without resentment.
There are no conflicts
    because no one will contend.

Daodejing 66

241

Excellence does not deceive.
Deception is not excellence.

Daodejing 81

242

I have three treasures:
First is kindness.
Second is moderation.
Third is never trying
to be first under heaven.

Kindness leads to boldness.
Moderation leads to vastness.
Never trying to be first under heaven
means one can be
a complete instrument of the eternal.

For those who reject
being kind for being bold,
being sparing for being vast,
being behind for being first:
    fatal!

For those who truly accept
that kindness will win, even in battle,
heaven will rescue them
and protect them with kindness.

Daodejing 67

13

修煉

Self-Cultivation

243

Know what's enough
   and you'll never be ashamed.
Know when to stop
   and you'll never be in danger.
That's the way to live long.

Daodejing 44

244

I was an official so long—it wore me out.
I'm glad to be exiled to the southern wilds,
to be an idle neighbor of gardeners and farmers
with the looks of someone from mountain woods.
I plow at dawn, turn dewy grass under;
row at night, oar echoing on creek rock.
I meet no one as I go forth and back:
singing long and loud to the azure sky.

"Living by a Creek," Liu Zongyuan (773–819)

245

Clouds rising in the sky
give us the image of waiting.
A noble one drinks
and feasts with joy.

Yijing, Image of hexagram 5: Waiting

246

Lofty and high, Taihua looms over Xianjing.
Heaven-made: no mortal could carve three peaks.
Clouds part before the Martial Emperor's Shrine.
Rain on the Immortal's Palm begins to clear.
The Qin Pass guards rivers and peaks to the north.
On the post road west running to the Han Altar,
travelers ask directions. They seek profit and fame—
but none of them stays to learn of long life.

"Passing Huayin," Cui Hao (704?–754)

247

Even an iron bar can be ground into a needle.

Proverb

248

Stand on tiptoe,
>and you won't stand firm.
Straddle wide,
>and you won't walk.
Display yourself,
>and you won't shine.
Assert yourself,
>and you won't be heeded.
Vaunt yourself,
>and you won't have merit.
Favor yourself,
>and you won't last long.

From the view of Tao,
>these are just crumbs and dregs,
>which no one likes.
Thus, no one with Tao
>acts in those ways.

>*Daodejing* 24

249

Wind moving in the sky
is the image of small taming.
A noble one values culture and virtue.

>*Yijing*, Image of hexagram 9: Smallness Tames

250

In my forest place, I worry about ebbing spring.
even though all looks splendid from my open pavilion.
Suddenly, a bluebird seems to call to me
and it invites me to the house of Red Pine.

The elixir is on the stove; he's just starting the first firing.
Immortal peaches ripened just after flowering
will impart a youthful coloring that will last.
How we cherish a drunkenness that flows like red clouds!

> "Qingming Feast at the Home of the Plum Flower Taoist Priest,"
> Meng Haoran (689/691–740)

251

The greatest calamity
  is not to know what is enough.
The greatest mistake
  is to want more.

Therefore:
  know when enough is enough
  and you'll always have enough.

> *Daodejing* 46

252

Favor and shame
are both fearful.
Honor and suffering
go with having a self.

Why do we say favor and shame
are both fearful?
Favor builds from the low,
so getting it leads to fear.
Thus we say that favor and shame
are both to be feared.

Why do we say that gain and suffering
go with having a self?
The reason I have great suffering
is that I have a body.
If I didn't have a body,
then how would I suffer?

Therefore, those who honor
the world as much as themselves
can further it.
Those who love
the world as much as themselves
can be trusted with it.

Daodejing 13

253

We look for what can't be seen—
  that's called invisible.
We listen for what can't be heard—
  that's called inaudible.
We grasp for what can't be touched—
  that's called intangible.

Each of these three modes
eludes our questions
even if we combine them into one.

> *Daodejing* 14

254

Close the portals,
  shut the gates,
  and all your life will be without toil.
Open the portals,
  busy yourself with wants,
  and all your life will be without safety.

> *Daodejing* 52

255

I reach my utmost emptiness
and guard my still depths.
I watch their cycles
as all things flourish together.

To know all people and creatures
would be like sorting tangled grass,
and yet each blade could be traced back to a root.
Returning to each root, we find stillness
and a repeating impulse.

This repeating impulse is constant:
knowledge of constancy is enlightenment;
ignorance of such constancy
is folly and evil.

Daodejing 16

256

Tao gives life,
virtue fosters.
They eternally give birth,
shelter from harm,
nurture and protect.

Daodejing 51

End learning and there will be no grief.
Between "ah" and "hem,"
how much difference is there between the two?
Between good and bad,
how do we choose between them?
What all people fear has to be feared.
And yet we still don't know what to do!
Everyone looks satisfied and pleased,
as if enjoying a great banquet,
or as if climbing to a terrace in spring.
I am alone, not knowing what's ahead,
like an infant who isn't yet grown,
or like one worn and bleak
with no home to return to.
Everyone has more than enough—
I alone seem to have lost it all.
Mine is a stupid man's heart!
I'm in chaos and confusion!
I'm the only one in darkness!
Normal people are clever and sure
while I am all out to sea,
buffeted by ceaseless winds!
Everyone has their places.
I alone am stubborn and glum.
I alone am different from other people:
I value succor from Mother.

Daodejing 20

258

Know manly strength,
but keep feminine softness.
Be the ravine of the world.
　　If you are the ravine of the world,
　　you'll never lose constant virtue
　　and you'll go back to being an infant.

Know the white,
but keep the black.
Be the model for the world.
　　If you are the model for the world,
　　you'll never err in constant virtue
　　and you'll return to the limitless.

Daodejing 28

259

To know others is wisdom
To know oneself is enlightened.
To overcome others takes strength.
To overcome oneself is might.
To be contented is wealth.
To move with vigor takes will.

He who does not lose will endure.
He who dies yet remains is long-lived.

Daodejing 33

260

As soon as you're born, you start to die.

Three in ten are the followers of life.
Three in ten are the followers of death.
Three in ten are alive, but going
toward the place of death.
> Why is that?
> Once they're born, they want to survive.

I've heard it said that the good preserve life
and can travel without meeting rhinoceros or tiger,
or go to battle without armor or weapons.
The rhinoceros will have no place to thrust its horn.
The tiger will have no place to slash its claws.
The warriors will have no place to stick their blades.
> Why is that?
Because the good have no place of death.

Daodejing 50

261

To have faults and not correct them
is to truly be at fault.

Proverb

262

Quick perception
is the flower of Tao,
and is the beginning of folly.
This is why a great person
dwells in the solid
and rejects the flimsy.
They keep with the fruit
and not the flower;
we must reject one to take the other.

Daodejing 38

263

To know what you don't know is superior.
Not to know what you don't know is illness.
Since people know illness as illness,
they want to remain well.

The sage is not ill,
and knows illness as illness,
and therefore remains well.

Daodejing 71

264

Whoever really cherishes Tao
is like a child.
Wasps, scorpions, and snakes won't bite,
fierce beasts won't pounce,
and raptors won't strike.
A child's bones and muscles are soft,
but the grasp is firm.
Not yet knowing the union of male and female,
yet each organ is complete and filled with vigor.

Crying all day without becoming hoarse
shows full harmony.
Knowing harmony is constancy.
Knowing constancy is clarity.
But to try to improve upon life is a bad sign.

The heart uses the body's energy, and that's called strength.
Whatever grows strong grows old;
we call that going against Tao.
Whatever goes against Tao
comes to an early end.

Daodejing 55

修煉

265

To see the small is clear,
to guard the soft is strength.
Those who use their light well
return to the clear
and won't lose themselves to distress.
This is to know the absolute.

Daodejing 52

14

Sageliness

266

In the first age, people didn't know
    they had rulers.
In the next age,
    they loved and praised them.
In the next,
    they revered them.
In the next,
    they despised them.

Trust could not be regained
and so mistrust followed
for such a long time!

How sparing with words
those earliest rulers were!
When the work was done,
people all said,
"We did it naturally!"

Daodejing 17

267

Earth, the powerful,
is the image of the feminine.
A noble one uses their great virtue
to support all beings.

Yijing, Image of hexagram 2: Earth

268

Understand constant tolerance:
Tolerance leads to community.
Community leads to leadership.
Leadership leads to heaven.
Heaven leads to Tao.
Tao leads to the everlasting.
To the end of your days,
know this and there will be no harm.

Daodejing 16

269

A gushing mountain spring
is the image of youth.
A noble one is fruitful and active
when teaching virtue.

Yijing, Image of hexagram 4: Youth

270

Accordingly, the wise carry out all matters
    without trying for their own results.
They teach without using words,
    let all things flourish without instruction,
    and let them grow without trying to own them.

Daodejing 2

聖
人

271

Wind below the mountain
is the image of poison.
A noble one rouses the people
to learn virtue.

Yijing, Image of hexagram 18: Poison

272

To act with strength is to comprehend power.
To comprehend power is to practice thoroughly until you
    reach the essence.
Memorize this, know this, analyze it.
Gradually, you'll reach the stage of doing as you please.
From the start, give up what others say you should do.

Shanxi Wang Zongyue's Taijiquan Treatise

273

Everyone dislikes
being abandoned, lonely, and unworthy,
and yet this is what kings call themselves.

And so some things are increased by being diminished,
while others are diminished by being increased.

Daodejing 42

274

Water on the earth
is the image of joining.
The ancient kings
built ten thousand nations
and stayed close to their leaders.

Yijing, Image of hexagram 8: Joining

275

Not singling some out as better
    will keep people from fighting.
Not prizing goods as costly and rare
    will keep people from stealing.
Not showing what stokes desire
    will keep hearts from tangling.

Daodejing 3

276

Thunder exploding to shake the earth
is the image of ease.
Be like the ancient kings
who made music praising virtue
as they made their many offerings to god,
and as they faced their ancestors' judgment.

聖人

Yijing, Image of hexagram 16: Delight

277

Heaven and earth are impartial:
　　they treat all things like straw dogs.
Sages are impartial:
　　they treat all people like straw dogs.

Daodejing 5

278

Thunder and lightning arriving
is the image of plenty.
A noble one knows
when to break relations
and apply the laws.

Yijing, Image of hexagram 55: Plenty

279

Therefore, the good person
is the teacher of the bad,
and the bad person
is the lesson for the good.
If one does not honor the teacher,
and if the teacher does not love the lesson,
then knowledge will go astray.
That is called the important secret.

Daodejing 27

聖
人

280

Earth by the lake
is the image of meeting.
A noble one never tires of teaching thought
and never stops protecting the people.

Yijing, Image of hexagram 19: Arrival

281

Brightness doubled
is the image of brilliance.
Great people increase their brilliance
and shine in four directions.

Yijing, Image of hexagram 30: Brilliance

282

The five colors make us blind.
The five tones make us deaf.
The five flavors dull our taste.
Hurry, haste, and pursuit
make our hearts go wild.
Coveting rare goods
hobbles our walk.

Therefore, wise people provide
for bellies and not eyes.
They leave one and choose the other.

Daodejing 12

283

Bent becomes whole.
Crooked becomes straight.
Empty becomes full.
Worn becomes new.
Few becomes many.
Many becomes confused.
  Therefore, the sages embrace unity
  and model it for the world.

Daodejing 22

284

Thus, when Tao is lost, morality follows.
When kindness is lost, justice follows.
When justice is lost, propriety follows.
  Such propriety is weak on loyalty and trust
  and is the start of disorder.

Daodejing 38

285

They don't show themselves,
  and yet they are bright.
They don't present themselves,
  and yet they are there.
They don't boast of themselves,
  and yet they do their work.
They don't favor themselves,
  and so they last long.

It is only because they are free of conflict
  that no one in the world conflicts with them.

Daodejing 22

286

Water overflowing
is the image of pit after pit.
A noble one moves with constant virtue,
and teaches duty again and again.

Yijing, Image of hexagram 29: Pit

287

Without walking out your door,
know all under heaven.

Without looking out of your window
see the Tao of heaven.

The farther you travel,
the less you know.

The sages were wise
without running around:

They named without seeing.
They finished without doing.

Daodejing 47

288

Wise people have no fixed hearts,
but take the hearts of the people as their own.

To those who are good to me,
    I am good.
To those who are bad to me,
    I am also good.
    That's good virtue.
To those who are sincere to me,
    I am sincere.
To those who are insincere to me,
    I am also sincere.
That's sincere virtue.

The wise people are at peace with the world
    and they keep their hearts obscure.
But the people keep their eyes and ears on them,
    and the wise people treat everyone as their children.

   Daodejing 49

289

The sage treats all the world as one family
and the nations as one people.

      Book of Rites, "Li Yun"

290

You can try to rule by being correct,
you can try to be crafty and use armed might,
but not to meddle is the right way to rule the world.
How do I know that is so?
By these:
    Too many threatening restrictions in the world
    make the people poorer.
    The more the tools of profit,
    the more the nation and clans go toward darkness.
    The more people are scheming and clever,
    the more laws and regulations multiply
    but the more crime and betrayal there are.

Daodejing 57

291

Thus, the worthy put their root in the base.
What is lofty has its foundation below.
That's why the rulers called themselves
"orphans," "insignificant," and "undeserving."
Wasn't it true that their root
was in the base? Isn't that so?
Therefore, what counts in eminence
is no praise.

Daodejing 39

292

It's always been difficult to attain perfect humaneness.
Only a sage can do it.
Thus, the noble person does not worry those
     who cannot do it,
nor do they shame those who cannot do it.
Thus, when the sages create a system of conduct,
they do not use themselves as the standards.
Instead, they give the people instructions,
encouraging a conscience,
so that people will feel abashed on their own
if they do not follow the words.

Book of Rites, "Biao Ji"

293

The ancestral temple is orderly and grand.
     A noble person built it.
The great plan is orderly and wise.
     The sages left nothing out.
They know the capacity
     of the hearts of others.
How the cunning hare skips and jumps
     only to be caught by the hound.

Book of Poetry, "Qiao Yan"

294

The noble ones are in awe of three things:
They are in awe of the will of heaven.
They are in awe of great people.
They are in awe of the words of the sages.

Petty people don't know the will of heaven
and so they have no awe.
They disrespect great people,
and they mock the words of the sages.

Analects, "Ji Shi"

295

How great is the sages' Tao!
Like the great oceans, it sends forth all things and beings,
and rises to the height of heaven!
It is excellent and superior in its greatness.
With three hundred times the just propriety,
and three thousand times righteous power,
it only needs people to walk that path.

Book of Rites, "Zhong Yong"

When Confucius climbed the eastern hills,
the country of Lu looked small.
When he climbed Mount Tai,
all the world looked small.

Thus, one who has seen the oceans
finds it hard to think of mere water.
One who has traveled to the gates of the sages
finds it hard to think of any other words.

There is an art to contemplating water:
one must contemplate the waves.
　　The sun and moon are bright
　　even when shining through shapes.

The characteristic of water
is that it must fill all hollows before flowing on.
　　When a noble person is intent on Tao,
　　they succeed only by understanding every part.

　　Mengzi, "Jin Xin I"

297

The teachings come from the Heaven's Tao,
and so the sages reach virtue.

　　Book of Rites, "Li Qi"

298

If government is slight,
the people stay simple and honest.
If government is oppressive,
then the people stay restless and poor.

聖人

Disaster!
    Happiness comes with it.
Happiness!
    Disaster hides in it.
Who knows which one
will ultimately occur?

Better not to try to correct.
Correction turns to deceit.
Goodness becomes sinister.
People have been caught
on this point for quite some time.

So the wise person is upright
and hurts no one,
is straight and never indulgent,
and bright but never dazzling.

Daodejing 58

299

In regulating important matters,
it is best to be spare.
Only by being spare can one forestall.
Forestalling strongly accumulates virtue.
Strongly accumulated virtue overcomes all.
Overcoming all leads to unlimited knowledge.
Only one with unlimited knowledge
is fit to rule a nation.
The ruler of a nation is its Mother
and can then endure.
So it's said that a deep root
is a solid base.
A long life requires
a long view of Tao.

Daodejing 59

300

When people don't fear authority,
great oppression descends.

Don't despise their homes.
Don't detest their lives.

If you avoid such rejection,
you won't be rejected in turn.

Daodejing 72

301

Ruling a big nation is like frying a small fish.
Manage the world through Tao
and demons will lose their power.
It's not that the demons really lose their power;
it's just that they will no longer hurt people.

But it's not just that they will no longer hurt people,
it's that the sage will not hurt people either.

When the two no longer fight each other,
then all virtue comes back together.

Daodejing 60

302

Therefore, the wise want no-wants.
They don't prize what's hard to get.
They learn to unlearn,
and return to what others pass by.
They help all creatures return to their natures
without daring to add anything of their own.

Daodejing 64

303

A great nation should be like flowing downhill,
the gathering place of the world,
the woman of the world.

As a woman always conquers the male with stillness—
a downward stillness—
so great nations must reach down to smaller ones
and thereby conquer them.
In turn, the smaller states,
by being below the great state,
will conquer the great state.

One conquers by becoming low,
the other conquers by staying low.

A great nation should want only to shelter people.
A small state should want only to be sheltered.
Both will get what they want,
as long as the great places itself low.

> *Daodejing* 61

304

Better to be flawed jade than a perfect stone.

> Proverb

305

Wise people know themselves
and so don't show themselves.
They love themselves
and yet don't boast of themselves.
They get rid of one mode
to take the other.

Daodejing 72

306

But people don't know this
and they don't know me.
Few know of me,
yet I am worthy.

Sages dress in rags
but have hearts of jade.

Daodejing 70

307

Wisdom isn't broad.
Breadth is not wise.

Daodejing 81

15 和平 Peace

308

When the world has Tao,
race horses pull night-soil carts.

When the world loses Tao,
war horses breed in the fields.

Daodejing 46

309

Cicadas chirp in bare mulberry woods.
In this eighth month, the road and pass are desolate.
Patrols come and go at the border checkpoint—
but yellow reeds and grass are everywhere.

Each of us ordered to be stationed here
has grown old facing the battlefield.
Don't learn to be like the warriors
who boast how good they are with dark horses.

"Song above the Border Pass," Wang Changling (698–756)

310

A good warrior
is not martial.
    A good fighter
    is never angry.
A good victor
never engages.
    A good commander
    remains subordinate.

So we say:
    virtue does not fight,
    strength commands well,
    the ultimate is to
    blend with perpetual heaven.

Daodejing 68

311

A lake gathering on the earth
is the image of collecting.
A noble one repairs the tools of war
against the unforeseen.

Yijing, Image of hexagram 45: Collecting

312

Power comes from the waist and hips.
Be mindful of change and turn, empty and full.
Let the breath-energy flow throughout your body without
deficiency.
Movement is in stillness, stillness is in movement,
miraculously forcing the opponent to adjust.

和
平

> *Shanxi Wang Zongyue's Taijiquan Treatise,* "The Song of Practicing
> the Thirteen Dynamics"

313

An arrogant army will always lose.

> Proverb

314

If the left becomes heavy, then make the left empty.
If the right becomes heavy, them make the right vanish.
If others try to reach up for me, then they must go higher.
If others try to reach down for me, then they must go lower.
If they advance, then the farther they have to go.
If they try to retreat, then the more pressed they will feel.

> *Shanxi Wang Zongyue's Taijiquan Treatise*

315

The bright moon lifts from heaven's peak;
a boundless haze between cloud and sea.
Ten thousand miles of endless wind
blasts its way through Jade Gate Pass.

Han troops marched on Baideng Road.
Hu troops stole into Qinghai Lake.
From the start, the battleground
never saw anyone return.

Soldiers gaze across the border,
their faces bitter, and think of home,
where tonight those in high towers
sigh and fail to find any rest.

"Moon over the Mountain Pass," Li Bai (701–762)

316

Water in the middle of the earth
is the image of armies.
A noble one gathers people together
and nourishes the multitude.

Yijing, Image of hexagram 7: Armies

317

Last year, you were sent to attack the Yuezhi:
your army vanished beyond the city walls.
Now the border is sealed and all news has stopped.
Are you dead, or alive, or wandering forever?
No one found even an abandoned tent
or knew of a returning horse with a torn flag.
Ceremonies are useless if I don't know where you are.
You're at the end of the world; I'm here crying.

"To a Friend Lost in the Tibetan War," Zhang Ji (766–830?)

和平

318

The world in chaos, we fled south together.
Now those times are over, and you go north alone.
My hair turns white in this foreign land.
In the capital again, you'll see our green hills.
The moon will rise across battered ramparts,
a millions stars will set over the pass,
and shivering animals in withered grass
on every side will accompany my worried face.

"Farewell to a Friend Returning North after the Rebellion Is
Quelled," Sikong Shu (720?–790?)

319

Strategists say:
    "I dare not be the host,
    but prefer to be the guest.
    I dare not advance by inches,
    but prefer to retreat by feet."

This is called movement
    without movement,
    seizing without arms,
    throwing without resistance,
    advancing before enemies appear.

Calamity is going lightly to war—
    how much would I lose
    that is precious to me?

Therefore, when armies clash,
    those who mourn will win.

Daodejing 69

320

A mountain rising from the earth
is the image of splitting.
The high are generous
to the low so all can live in peace.

Yijing, Image of hexagram 23: Splitting

321

I see that anyone
who wants to conquer the world
will never succeed.

The world is a sacred vessel
no one can possess.
Those who try will be defeated.
Those who grab for it will lose it.

Some things move forward, some follow behind.
　　Some blow hot, some blow cold.
Some are strong, some are weak.
　　Some may chop, some may fall.

That's why the sage
　　avoids the excessive,
　　avoids the extravagant,
　　and avoids the exalted.

　　　Daodejing 29

322

A lake below a mountain
is the image of decrease.
A noble one holds their anger
and curbs their desires.

　　　Yijing, Image of hexagram 41: Decrease

323

A mountain under the sky
is the image of distance.
A noble one stays far from the vile,
does not attack, and yet is firm.

Yijing, Image of hexagram 33: Withdrawal

324

What others teach,
I also teach:
the violent and strong do not die naturally.
That is the basis of my teaching.

Daodejing 42

325

Fire burning over wood
is the image of the cauldron.
A noble one takes the right seat
and sets their commands.

Yijing, Image of hexagram 50: Cauldron

However beautiful, weapons
are tools of ill omen,
hateful to all beings.
Those who have Tao don't use them.

The prince usually values the left,
but values the right when using troops.
Armies are tools of ill omen
and they are not the tools of a prince.
They are used only as a last resort.

Calm and repose are better.
Force is not beautiful.
To call it beautiful
is to delight in killing people.
Those who kill people
can never carry out the will of the world.

Celebration proceeds on the left.
Mourning proceeds on the right.
The lieutenant stands on the left.
The high general stands on the right,
in the place of mourning.
He is the killer of multitudes.
Mourning, grief, and sobbing surround him.
For he, the victor in war, hands out funerals.

Daodejing 31

327

Don't take fish from the depths.
Whatever benefits a state
should be revealed to no one.

Daodejing 36

和平

328

Fire over water
is the image of not-yet-across.
A noble one sorts things with care
and puts them in their rightful places.

Yijing, Image of hexagram 64: Not Yet Across

329

A moment of patience avoids a hundred days of regret.

Proverb

330

Wind above a lake
is the image of inner faith.
A noble one mediates lawsuits
and is slow to execute.

Yijing, Image of hexagram 61: Inner Confidence

331

If I were to tell everyone
to follow the great Tao,
I would be afraid
of what they would do.

The great Tao is straightforward,
but people like detours.

When the official courts are well kept,
    the fields are barren
    and the granaries are empty.
When officials wear elegant silks,
    dangle sharp swords,
    pamper themselves with food and drink,
    and heap overflowing property and wealth,
    they are called arrogant thieves.
That is the corruption of Tao!

     Daodejing 53

332

Thunder and wind
are the image of constancy.
A noble one stands firm
and does not change direction.

      Yijing, Image of hexagram 32: Constancy

333

One who relies on strong armies does not conquer.
A strong tree will be chopped down.

Daodejing 76

334

Resentment will still linger
even when peace follows hatred,
so how can we make good on peace?

A wise person holds an exact tally
but doesn't hold others exactly to it.
Use virtue to manage agreements,
because pettiness is vicious.

Heaven's Tao is impartial
and always helps good people.

Daodejing 79

335

Thunder exploding in the sky
is the image of innocence.
The ancient kings
followed the seasons
and nourished all creatures.

Yijing, Image of hexagram 25: Innocence

Let a small country
keep a small population,
and have a supply of goods
ten- or a hundredfold more
than people can use.
Let the people be serious about death
and not migrate far.

While they would have boats and carts,
they wouldn't ride them.
While they would have armor and weapons,
they wouldn't show them.

Let them return to
tallying with knotted cords,
sweet food,
beautiful clothes,
restful dwellings,
and joyful customs.

Let neighboring countries see each other,
and hear one another's chickens and dogs,
but to old age,
even to death,
let no state invade another.

Daodejing 80

和平

337

Nature says little:
A cyclone doesn't last beyond a morning.
A downpour doesn't last beyond a day.
Who does this?
Heaven and earth.
If heaven and earth can't last long,
that's even more true of our own actions!

Daodejing 23

338

Therefore, when it comes to matters of Tao,
    join those with Tao,
    join those with virtue,
    join those with loss.

For those with Tao
    have the joy of joining with it.
Those with virtue
    have the joy of joining with it.
Those with loss
    have the joy of joining with it.
But those without faith
    will have no faith from others.

Daodejing 22

339

Tao gives life,
virtue fosters it,
things take form,
and power is complete.
That's why every creature
reveres Tao and values virtue.

When Tao is revered
and virtue valued,
> then everyone naturally
> obeys it always.

Daodejing 51

340

Therefore, Tao is great.
Heaven is great.
Earth is great.
The king is also great.
In this world, there are these Four Greats,
and the king is one of them.

Human law follows the earth.
Earth's law follows heaven.
Heaven's law follows Tao.
Tao's law is nature.

Daodejing 25

16 無為 Nonaction

341

All will grow without anyone saying so,
bringing all results without anyone's orders.
All work is done without anyone doing it:
this will never go away.

Daodejing 2

342

Orchid leaves, lush in spring.
Splendid cassias, bright autumn.
All the blooms are at their vital peak,
each one is the season's glory.
Could a forest hermit know
the pleasure of these scented winds?
Plants have their own root-hearts:
why ask a beauty to pluck them out?

"Lament 2," Zhang Jiuling (673–740)

343

The sages ruled by opening hearts,
filling bellies, soothing wills,
and strengthening bones.
They always kept the people
free of thought or desires—
for where there was thought
the cunning were sure to act on it.
When there were no such deeds,
then all was peaceful.

Daodejing 3

344

The action that spoils
and the seizing that brings loss
are actions sages avoid
and so they are never defeated.
They neither spoil nor seize.
But most people chase their affairs
and constantly ruin them before they're done.
If they were as careful in ending
as they were in beginning,
they wouldn't ruin what they did.

Daodejing 64

345

Master, what did you achieve
by persisting in your era?
Zou clan villages dot the land.
The Palace of Lu is where your home was.
You sighed when no phoenix appeared
and knew that you had reached your end.
When a unicorn was found wounded,
you knew that your Tao was through.
Today, gazing between these two pillars,
I make my offering and libation to you:
as in a dream, our times seem to be the same.

> "Passing through the State of Lu and Sighing While Offering a
> Sacrifice to Confucius," Tang Xuanzong (Emperor Xuanzong of
> Tang; 685–792)

346

Thunder above the lake
is the image of the marrying sister.
A noble one understands the long term
and yet knows the hazards.

> *Yijing*, Image of hexagram 54: Marrying Sister

Act without acting.
Work without working.
Taste without tasting.
Enlarge the small by multiplying the small.
Repay hatred with kindness.

Deal with the difficult while all is easy.
Deal with the big while all is tiny.
All difficult matters in the world
surely began from the easy.
All great matters in the world
surely began from the tiny.

Therefore, the sage doesn't deal with problems
when they're big
and so has great accomplishments,
while those who makes careless promises surely lose trust
and those who only want ease will have much difficulty.

This is how the sage deals with difficulty,
and so in the end has no difficulties.

Daodejing 63

348

Wood growing from the earth
is the image of rising.
A noble one is mild in their virtue
as they heap the small
into the high and big.

       Yijing, Image of hexagram 46: Rising

349

You can easily hold what lies still.
You can easily forestall what isn't here yet.
You can easily break what's brittle.
You can easily scatter what's small.
Act before things are at hand.
Sort before disorder occurs.
A tree big enough to embrace
grows from a tiny shoot.
A nine-story tower
rises from a heap of dirt.

       Daodejing 64

350

Nonbeing enters where there is no space.
I know that nonaction has its advantage.

       Daodejing 43

351

When learning, increase every day.
    For Tao, decrease every day.
Decrease, and decrease again
    until you reach not-doing.

Not-doing does everything.
Keep with what's constant in the world
    and you'll have no trouble.
But if you grab at trouble,
    you won't get anything in the world.

Daodejing 48

352

The ancients who followed Tao well
did not try to "enlighten" people.
Instead, they urged innocence.
The challenge of governing people
comes from too much knowledge.
Knowledge in ruling a nation
only ruins it.
Innocence in ruling a nation
brings blessings.
Know the difference
and make it your standard.

Daodejing 65

353

Those of high virtue never act,
    yet all is done.
Those of lower virtue act,
    and fallout follows.
Those of great kindness
    cause no issues.
Those of great justice
    cause backlash.
Those of great propriety bare their arms
    to force their rules on others.

Daodejing 38

354

Sages don't accumulate.
When they do for others,
    they do more for themselves.
When they give to others,
    they give more to themselves.

Daodejing 81

17

無

Nothingness

355

The space between heaven and earth—
    isn't it like a bellows?
Empty without bending,
    the more it moves,
    the more it puts out.

Daodejing 5

356

Leaves fall constantly and mix with evening rain.
I comfort myself by singing "Red Silk" aloud.
My feelings are full, but I don't mind being friendless.
I cultivate emptiness and throw suffering on the waves.
The carriages of old men are heard outside my gates.
Taoist scrolls are piled up beside my pillow.
In the end, plain people go to the cloudy heavens—
green water, blue mountains, transcended in one time.

"Worried Thoughts," Yu Xuanji (844–869)

357

Wind blowing over water
is the image of spreading.
The ancient kings
made offerings to god
and built temples.

無

> *Yijing*, Image of hexagram 59: Spreading

358

I enter the ancient temple in early morning.
as the rising sun grazes the high trees.
I follow a twisting path to a secluded place
where a meditation hall is surrounded by flowering woods.

The mountain light stirs the delighted birds.
My heart is as empty as this reflecting pool.
Ten thousand sounds become completely still:
all that's heard is the bell that rings the hours.

> "Inscription behind the Meditation Hall of Poshan Temple,"
> Chang Jian (708–765)

359

Don't fear slowing; fear stopping.

> Proverb

360

Tao courses by using the empty.
So deep! It seems to be
the ancestor of all things!

Daodejing 4

361

The space between heaven and earth—
    isn't it like a bellows?
Empty without bending,
    the more it moves, the more it puts out.

Daodejing 5

362

You came from the east to visit me,
the rain of Baling still on your clothes.
I ask why you have come, and you say:
"To buy an ax to chop mountain trees."
How deep and steady the flowers bloom.
How fledgling swallows swoop and soar.
Yesterday is gone, and now it's spring.
Look how white our temples have turned!

"Meeting Feng Zhe in Chang'an," Wei Yingwu (737–792)

363

Mountain monks sit playing chess.
Above the game, bamboo shadows clear.
No one sees them among the bamboo—
they only hear the chess pieces click.

"By the Pond," Bai Juyi (772–846)

無

364

Autumn skies, a full moon again.
One night in-a-thousand at the city gate:
that's how we meet again in Jiangnan—
so unbelievable that it only happens in dreams.
Winds startle hidden magpies from the trees.
Insects shiver in the cold wet grass.
But travelers can always join in drinking wine:
lingering only in fear of the morning bell.

"Old Friends of the River Country Meeting by Chance and
Gathering at an Inn," Dai Shulin (732–789)

365

Thirty spokes join at one hub—
an entire cart depends
on that empty space.

Turn clay into a bowl—
its usefulness comes
from its empty space.

Cut doors and windows into a room,
that room is useful
because of those empty spaces.

Therefore, what is solid
may be beneficial,
but what is empty
is useful.

Daodejing 11

18

樸
素

Simplicity

366

To know contentment
is to be forever happy.

> *Proverb*

367

The northern slopes of Zhongnan are elegant,
with snow banks massed high in the clouds.
The woods stand brightly against the blue sky
while here in town the evenings grow cold.

> "Gazing at Snow on the Zhongnan Mountains,"
> Zu Yong (699–746?)

368

A bird doesn't sing to answer.
It sings because it wants to sing.

> Proverb

369

The good scholars of ancient times
knew the small, the subtle,
the mysterious, and the coursing.
They were deeper than we could know
and most people didn't understand them.

This is how they looked:
Relaxed! Like those fording a winter stream.
Undecided! Like those with danger all around.
Grave! Like those with great dignity.
Expansive! Like melting ice.
Honest! Like raw wood.
Broad! Like a valley.
Murky! Like muddy water.

Who can still muddy waters
and let them settle into clarity?
Who can calm great force
into quiet growth?

Embrace this Tao, and don't try to overfill.
If you don't try to overfill, you are beyond
wearing out or renewal.

Daodejing 15

370

A lone swan rises from the sea.
It doesn't dare to land on the lake,
but angles toward two kingfishers,
nestled in a three-bead tree.
So brave at the top of that lush wood,
do they not fear the golden bullet?
Bright plumes draw pointed fingers,
high brilliance invites divine harm.
Now, I must travel far and deep,
never to be shot for a prize.

"Lament 1," Zhang Jiuling (673–740)

371

Peaceful thoughts, uninterrupted.
Sailing and following whatever comes.
The evening breeze blows my boat:
a flowered journey at the creek's mouth.
At the edge of night, I turn to West Valley:
gaze at Brother Mountains and the Dipper.
Everything dissolves in the lake mists.
Moon slants lower behind the woods.
Trouble swamps us everywhere:
be an old man with a fishing pole.

"Springtime Floating on Ruoye Creek," Qiwu Qian (692?–755?)

372

I sow beans under the south hill:
plenty of weeds, few sprouts.
Rising at dawn I tend the soil,
toting my hoe, I lead the moon home.
Grass and trees narrow the trail,
evening dew dampens my clothes.
But wet clothes don't matter
if nothing goes against my hopes.

樸
素

"Returning to Live on the Farm, 3," Tao Yuanming (365–427)

373

Those who talk do not know.
Those who know stay silent.
I heard this phrase from Lao Jun.
But if Lao Jun was one who knew,
why did he write five thousand words?

"Reading Laozi," Bai Juyi (772–846)

374

A beautiful lake
is the image of exchange
A noble one talks and studies with friends.

Yijing, Image of hexagram 58: Exchange

375

When we speak of using the body
and of guidelines for action,
the mind and breath-energy are the lords
and the blood and muscles are the subjects.
Full pushing uses the mind, but in the end,
where are we going?
To increase longevity,
to prolong life,
to avoid aging.

Shanxi Wang Zongyue's Taijiquan Treatise, "The Song of Practicing
the Thirteen Dynamics"

376

Know honor
but remember disgrace.
Be the valley of the world.
    If you are the valley of the world,
    you'll have enough constant virtue
    and you'll return to being like raw wood.

Raw wood is harvested to make tools,
just as the sage is used as a public servant
to create a great system
that never cuts anyone out.

Daodejing 28

377

End sageness, reject wisdom,
  and the people will benefit a hundredfold.
End benevolence, reject righteousness,
  and the people will return
  to being filial and kind.
End cleverness, reject profit,
  and robbers and thieves will vanish.

All three patterns fall short.

This is all we've ever needed:
  see plainly;
  hold simplicity;
  check the selfish;
  reduce desire.

Daodejing 19

378

Thunder in the middle of the lake
is the image of following.
A noble one feasts and rests
when night falls.

Yijing, Image of hexagram 17: Following

379

Tao never does, yet everything is done.
If lords and kings could keep it,
everything would be transformed by itself.
Once changed and rising,
it is the nameless simplicity of restraint.
Nameless simplicity
acts without intention,
with no desires, and in stillness.
Then the world will settle by itself.

Daodejing 37

380

Therefore, wise people say:

I will do nothing
    and the people will reform themselves.
I will stay tranquil,
    and the people will correct themselves.
I will make no trouble,
    and the people will grow rich by themselves.
I will have no ambitions,
    and the people will be simple by themselves.

Daodejing 57

Glossary and Notes

Understanding the references often enhances the understanding of the material. Poets often used alternate or ancient names for various locations, and some places have been renamed over the thousands of years. In addition, famous people are mentioned, and it helps to know who they are. Some basic notes on the translations are below, followed by a glossary of important words, and a brief description of major sources.

- In Chinese, the family name, or surname, comes first. For example, Li Bai is from the Li family.
- All Chinese has been transliterated according to the pinyin system. The only exceptions are *Tao* (Dao) and *Confucius* (Kong Fuzi), because those terms are commonly known by such long-standing spellings.
- When a geographical or formal name has a relevant meaning, it is given as part of the definition. However, in some cases, geographical and proper nouns originated as a local pronunciation that was codified later with a similar-sounding written word. In other cases, names from a foreign language were translated phonetically into Chinese. For those words, no literal meaning is given.
- Dates before the common era (BCE) are noted as such. Otherwise, all dates are in the common era (CE).

Anxi   "The Pacified West," this is a reference to Anxi Duhufu, located in present-day Kuqa County, Xinjiang Uyghur Autonomous Region. In 663, the khan of the Western Turks surrendered the territory to the Tang and the area was put under the administration of a military commissioner.

Baideng Road   The Battle of Baideng was a military conflict between the Han Dynasty and the Xiongnu (a confederation of nomadic peoples from the eastern Asian steppes) in 200 BCE.

Baling The former name of Yueyang, a present-day city in Hunan Province. It is situated on the east bank of the Xiangjiang River, which flows from Dongting Lake, close to where it joins the Yangzi River.

Beigu Mountain Literally, "Northern Fortress," Beigu Mountain is in Zhenjiang, Jiangsu Province. It faces the Yangzi River.

Bluebird Mentioned in "Qingming Feast at the Home of the Plum Flower Taoist Priest," by Meng Haoran (p. 112), the bluebird is a messenger of the goddess Xi Wangmu or the Queen Mother of the West.

Boyish Mentioned in "Qingming Feast at the Home of the Plum Flower Taoist Priest," by Meng Haoran (p. 112), this is a reference to the *tongzi,* or virgin child. Such a child was supposedly pure, unblemished by human society, and immortal.

breath-energy This represents the word *qi.* Qi means breath, energy, and stamina. A person has breath-energy. The classics also speak of the universe's energy as qi. We are in constant exchange with this universal energy as literally as breathing air, and the Taoist consider that all beings are animated by this universal qi.

Chang'an Literally meaning "Perpetual Peace," Chang'an was settled in Neolithic times and was the capital of more than ten dynasties. It is one terminus of the Silk Road. The city was renamed Xi'an in the Ming Dynasty and it is known by that name today.

Changshan Taoist *Changshan* means "the constant mountain," and the word *chang* is used frequently in the *Daodejing.*

Chu A state during the Zhou Dynasty (1046–256 BCE), Chu was founded c. 1030 BCE and conquered by the state of Qin in 223 BCE. Chu included most of the present-day provinces of Hubei and Hunan, along with parts of Chongqing, Guizhou, Henan, Anhui, Jiangxi, Jiangsu, Zhejiang, and Shanghai. Chu was Laozi's home state.

Confucius The name Confucius (551–479 BCE) is a Latinized form of Kong Fuzi, meaning "Master Kong." His personal name was Kong Qiu. He was a teacher, editor, statesman, and philosopher. He is traditionally credited as the author or editor of many Chinese classics, his thought shaped the whole of Chinese history for thousands of years, and his outlook is still a part of Chinese culture today. He had seventy-two major disciples.

dantian Meaning "field of elixir," the dantian is a point of meditative concentration in the lower abdomen, three fingers' widths below the level of the navel, and in the center of the body. *Elixir* is derived from the elixir of immortality. (See *elixir*.) When no effective physical elixir could be made, people turned to meditative means. The dantian is regarded as the source of the raw energy that is supposed to impart immortality. There are really three dantian: lower, middle (level of the solar plexus), and upper (level of eyebrows). If not specified, references are usually to the lower dantian.

Dayu Mountains A mountain range located between Guangdong and Jiangxi Provinces.

Dongting Lake A large lake in Hunan Province whose name means "Grotto Court." The lake is part of the flood basin of the Yangzi River. Two provinces have names that reference this lake—Hubei means "north of the lake," and Hunan means "south of the lake."

Double Nine Festival The name refers to the ninth day of the ninth lunar month. According to beliefs derived from the *Yijing,* nine is a yang number, so double nine is doubly yang. This gives rise to the alternate name, "Heavy Yang Festival." The festival's origin is related to guarding against pestilence. People will climb a high mountain, drink chrysanthemum liquor or tea, and wear cuttings of dogwood to escape disease. It is also an important time for family reunions and to visit ancestral graves.

Eight Trigrams The Eight Trigrams, or, in Chinese, the "Bagua," is an octagonal arrangement of trigrams (groupings of three lines apiece). A trigram is made up of some combination of either a straight line (representing yang) or a split line (representing yin). Yin and yang equals two, and 2^3 equals eight formations of every possible combination of yin and yang lines. Each trigram is a symbol: heaven, earth, water, fire, wind, thunder, lake, and mountain. The Eight Trigrams become a cosmological chart by arranging the trigrams in an octagonal formation.

elixir Called *dan* in Chinese, this is a reference to the elixir of immortality, which consisted of many rare and esoteric ingredients that had to be fired in a special crucible and stove for long periods. Mentioned in "Qingming Feast at the Home of the Plum Flower Taoist Priest," by Meng Haoran (p. 112).

Emei Mount Emei is one of the Four Sacred Buddhist Mountains of China and is located in Sichuan Province. It is traditionally regarded as the place of enlightenment of the bodhisattva Samantabhadra (Puxian Pusa). The first Buddhist temple was built there in the first century CE.

Fang, Grand Marshall Fang Guan (697–763) was an official of the Tang Dynasty (618–907) and served as chancellor to Emperor Xuanzong (685–762) and Emperor Suzong (711–762). Late in life, he was demoted and sent to low-ranking posts in the provinces, but was recalled to serve as minister of justice. He died during his return journey at a monastery in Langzhou (the capital of Gansu Province, northwestern China).

Five Phases Called Wu Xing and sometimes translated as the Five Elements, the Five Phases are wood, fire, earth, metal, and water. However, these should be considered symbols of types of changing movement rather than matter. Briefly, wood describes that which grows upward; fire, that which is hot, bright, expanding, and consuming; Earth, that which settles, balances, spreads out, and neutralizes; Metal, that which solidifies and grows hard; Water, that which liquefies, cools, and flows downward. The system came to maturity in the first or second century BCE during the Han Dynasty, and became the basis for thought in numerous parts of Chinese culture including cosmology, metaphysics, the calendar, traditional Chinese medicine, music, martial arts, the tea ceremony, and the dynastic traditions.

Four Mystical Animals Mentioned in the *Book of Rites,* "Applying Ritual," they are the Qilin (Chinese unicorn), phoenix, tortoise, and dragon.

Fuzhou The capital of Fujian Province. During the Tang Dynasty (618–907), political upheavals prompted a migration of people from the heartland to this coastal area. Prosperity grew and Buddhism was quickly adopted.

Gansu A province located in northwest China.

Great Peak In the poem "Gazing at the Peak" (p. 2), Du Fu is at the base of Mount Tai, or Taishan, located near the city of Tai'an, Shandong Province. It is the eastern member of the Five Sacred Mountains and is considered the first among them. It has been a place of worship and royal ceremony for at least 3,000 years.

Guangling A district in Yangzhou, Jiangsu Province. The distance between Yangzhou and Luoyang is far—about 783 km (487 mi) and if Wei Yingwu was traveling by boat in "Embarking on the Yangzi, Sending a Letter to Officer Yuan" (p. 14), the journey would have been against the current, and much of the route would have been over land.

Guanque Tower With a name that means "Stork Tower," this is one of the Four Famous Towers of China, and is located in the ancient city of Puzhou in Yongji, Shanxi.

Han (people) The major ethnic group of China, comprising about 92 percent of the population.

Han (river) A river known also as Hanshui or Han Jiang, it is the longest tributary of the Yangzi River. It mostly crosses Shaanxi and Hubei Provinces. The Han people and the Han Dynasty (206–220) take their names from it. The ideograph for *Han* combines the signs for water with one that means "yellow loam."

Han Altar A place where the emperors of Han made religious sacrifices.

Heaven In Chinese, this is the word *tian*, which also means "sky." It names the broadest, eternal, and supreme power in the world. Although it is regarded as having a will—its actions irresistibly change human and natural life—it is not a personage. It is not the residence of a god or gods nor a place for an afterlife. Although heaven is seen as the highest initiating power, it is not capable of doing everything on its own. That's why it must be paired with earth. What heaven initiates—weather, sun and moon, the seasons—earth must receive, nurture, and grow.

Heaven's Peak A reference to the Qilian Mountains, which divide Qinghai and Gansu Provinces. They are also known as the Tianshan Mountains, which literally means "Heaven's Mountains."

Hu This was a general term for non-Chinese people living to the north and northwest of China, as well as central Asia.

Huayin A city in Shaanxi Province. Its name means "North of Hua (mountain)" because yin is the shady side and therefore the north. In the poem "Passing Huayin" (p. 110), Cui Hao refers to people traveling to the capital of Chang'an to seek profit and fame, bypassing Hua Mountain where Taoists taught the ways of wellness and long life.

Huazhou A town and district in Shaanxi Province, east of Chang'an. In "Huazhou" (p. 47), we see Du Fu sorrowfully leaving the area. The rebellion referenced is the An Lushan Rebellion (755–763). In 756, rebels captured Chang'an forcing the emperor and his court to flee. Imperial forces and a new emperor did not recover the city until 757. The new court ousted Fang Guan (see the poem, in "Leaving the Grave of Grand Marshall Fang," p. 37), and as an ally of Fang's, Du Fu was demoted in 758 to serve as educational commissioner of Huazhou.

immortal The Chinese character combines the words for "person" and "mountain," thereby alluding to the remote places that the immortals were supposed to have lived. The idea of an immortal is specifically a Taoist concept, and it was believed that one could become an immortal by making and drinking the elixir of immortality, through meditative practices, or by good fortune. A significant part of the cult of immortals was the belief that an island of immortals named Penglai existed in the Pacific Ocean.

immortal peaches A bite of these legendary peaches grown by the goddess Xi Wangmu or the Queen Mother of the West, would grant long life. They are a traditional Taoist symbol mentioned in "Qingming Feast at the Home of the Plum Flower Taoist Priest," by Meng Haoran (p. 112).

Immortal's Palm A rock formation on Hua Mountain that looks like a gigantic palm print in the cliff.

Jade Gate Pass The Yumen Pass is a pass of the Great Wall west of Dunhuang in what is now northwest Gansu Province. The Silk Road passed through this point during the Han Dynasty (206–220).

Jiang In the poem "The Jiang and Han River" (p. 28), Jiang ("river") probably refers to the Yangzi River. Since the Han is a tributary of the Yangzi, this places Du Fu at the confluence of the two great bodies of water. The Yangzi River is considered a major dividing line between northern and southern China.

Jiangnan A reference to the lands south of the Yangzi River. It has long been one of the most prosperous and cultured regions of China due to its wealth of natural resources, rich history, and powerful cities. The region includes the southern parts of Jiangsu and Anhui Provinces, the northern part of Jiangxi Province, and the northern part of Zhejiang Province.

Jie, Emperor Ruler of the Xia Dynasty (1728 – 1675 BCE). He is regarded as a tyrant and oppressor.

junzi This originally meant a ruler or an aristocrat. It was soon expanded to mean a cultivated person who tried to perfect themselves and who would then be an exemplar for that same cultivated life in the world. Older translations use terms such as *gentleman* and *superior person*.

Lao Jun Translating to "Lord Lao," this is another name for Laozi, the author of the *Daodejing*. Laozi's deified name is Taishang Laojun, or "Supreme High Old Lord."

Laozi This honorific name means "Old Master" (sixth–fifth centuries BCE). His given name was Li Er; he was an archivist serving the Zhou dynasty, a philosopher, a teacher, and the author of the *Daodejing*.

Li Duan A native of Zhaozhou and another poet collected in *300 Tang Poems*, Li Duan (743–782) was a close friend of Lu Lun, as shown in the poem "Farewell to Li Duan" (p. 39).

Lintao This is present-day Minxian County, Gansu Province. During the Warring States (475–221 BCE) and the Qin Dynasty (221–207), sections of the Great Wall ran through this area.

Lu A vassal state during the Zhou Dynasty (1046–256 BCE), founded in the eleventh century BCE. Lu was the home state of Confucius.

Lumen Mountain A mountain southeast of Xiangyang City, Hubei Province. Its name translates to Deer Gate.

Luoyang One of the Four Ancient Capitals of China, Luoyang is situated on China's central plain, where the Luo and Yellow Rivers join. Its name means "The Sunny Bank of the Luo River," using the term *yang*, because the northern bank was always lit by sun from the south. The earliest settlements were established in Neolithic times. The first capital in the area was founded in 2070 BCE as the capital of the Xia Dynasty. The first Buddhist temple in China, the White Horse Temple, was built in 68 CE. During the Eastern Han Dynasty (25–220 CE), Luoyang was as a terminus to the Silk Road. In the Tang Dynasty (618–907), Luoyang was known as the Eastern Capital and its population of about one million was second only to Chang'an, which at that time was the largest city in the world.

Martial Emperor Emperor Wu of Han (141–87). Emperor Wu worshiped the Taoist divinity Tai Yi. The emperor built a "House of Longevity" (shou gong) chapel at his Ganquan palace complex in modern Xianyang, Shaanxi, and dedicated it to that god in 118 BC. Wudi was fascinated with immortality, and he associated with alchemists who were trying to find the elixir of immortality.

Master Chao's Temple When Liu Zongyuan wrote "Visiting Master Chao's Temple at Daybreak to Read a Zen Scripture" in 806 (p. 59), he had just been demoted and was living at the Longxing (Rising Dragon) Temple in Yongzhou, Hunan Province. The Liuzi Temple in Yongzhou was built as a memorial to the Tang poet Liu Zongyuan (773–819).

Mount Mang A mountain in Hubei Province.

Mount Meru In the poem "One Hundred Word Stela" (p. 23), Lu Dongbin references "Xu Mu," another term for Mount Meru. This is a Sanskrit name for a sacred cosmic mountain with five peaks. It is considered the center of the universe in Hindu, Jain, and Buddhist cosmology.

Nanshan Another name for the Zhongnan Mountain. Simply meaning "South Mountain," the term can also refer to other places, including mountains in Hubei or Gansu Provinces.

Nanxi There are two Nanxi ("Southern Creek") in China—one in Yunnan Province, and the other in Zhejiang Province. The places Liu Changqing refers to in "Searching Nanxi for the Reclusive Changshan Taoist" (p. 15) were closer to Zhejiang Province, and he's more likely to have visited there.

noble one See *junzi*.

Pang Gong Born in Xiangyang during the Eastern Han Dynasty (25–221). He and his wife became recluses rather than serve the provincial governor.

Poshan Temple This temple is now called the Xingfu Temple and is located in Changshu, Jiangsu Province. Ni Denguang, the magistrate of Chengzhou, Hunan province, donated his estate for a temple near the Polong Stream (Breaking Dragon stream) and so the temple was named Poshan (Broken Mountain) Temple. In 869 BCE the emperor gave the temple a large bell along with a board inscribed with "Xingfu Temple" ("Rising Fortune Temple"). The temple is proud of its association with Chang Jian's poem "Inscription behind the Meditation Hall of Poshan Temple" (p. 164). Their Empty Mind Pavilion takes its name from that work.

qin (musical instrument) Also called a *guqin* ("ancient zither"), the qin is a seven-stringed zither and is the premier instrument for the scholar, recluse, sage, and any cultivated person in classical Chinese society. It is fretless and is often played solo. The qin is considered to be the "father of all Chinese music" and the "instrument of the sages."

Qin (state) An ancient state during the Zhou Dynasty (1046–256 BCE) from the ninth century–221 BCE in the north and west of present-day China. In the third century BCE, under the leadership of Qin Shi Huangdi (259–210 BCE), Qin emerged as the most dominant state among the seven major warring states. By conquering all of them, Qin created the territory of what is roughly modern-day China.

Qin Pass A reference to Tongguan, a pass just east of Hua Mountain. In some contexts, it can refer to the Hangu Pass, which the Qin fortified in 361 BCE. Since Cui Hao is discussing scenes of Hua Mountain in "Passing Huayin" (p. 110), he's more likely referring to Tongguan.

Qinghai Lake The largest lake in the People's Republic of China, it is located in Qinghai Province. Its name, which means "Blue Ocean," describes its vivid color.

Qingming The festival day where families visit and clean the graves of their ancestors. Literally meaning "clear and bright," the day usually falls sometime in early April. By titling the poem "Qingming Feast at the Home of the Plum Flower Taoist Priest" (p. 112), Meng Haoran is deliberately setting a contrary scene with many images of Taoist immortality.

Quanjiao Mountain Located in Quanjiao County, Anhui Province.

Red Pine A direct translation of "Chi Song," he was a legendary Taoist immortal who was Lord of the Rain under Shennong (the Divine Husbandman, said to be born in the twenty-eighth century BCE). He is regarded as the inventor of the cart and plow, first tamer of the ox and horse, and advocate of clearing land with fire. He is also regarded as a pioneer of using medicinal herbs. Mentioned in

"Qingming Feast at the Home of the Plum Flower Taoist Priest" (p. 112), by Meng Haoran.

Ruoye Creek A stream in Shaoxing, Zhejiang Province.

sage The *shengren* is an enlightened and wise person. The word *sheng* combines the signs for "person" with the signs for "speech" and "listening." A sage is a person who is good at speaking and listening. China has a long tradition of positing a sage-king who is the ideal ruler. Paradoxically, such people always decline the appointment.

Shanyin A county in Shanxi, China.

Shu Another name for Sichuan Province, Shu refers to one of the Three Kingdoms to emerge after the fall of the Han Dynasty (206 BCE–220 CE). The state of Shu was established in 221 and was conquered in 263.

Shun Emperor Shun (r. 2233–2184 BCE) was a legendary emperor known for his humility and filial piety. He served under Emperor Yao in several important posts and was appointed as his successor. Shun declined at first, but Yao eventually abdicated his throne to him.

Son of Heaven Literally, the "child of heaven," this was a reference to the emperor.

South Mountain In "Returning at Year's End to South Mountain" (p. 53), by Meng Haoran, Nanshan may be Zhongnan Mountain in Shaanxi Province. Other sources assert that it was Meng's birth area, which would have placed it in Xiangyang in Hubei Province. The Qilian Mountains in Gansu Province are also known as South Mountain.

supreme ultimate This is the translation of "Taiji" and can also be interpreted as "the supreme limit." Taiji had an independent philosophical meaning long before it was borrowed as the name of the martial art. Taiji means yin and yang together. When Laozi wrote "one birthed two" (p. 11), the number two implies Taiji, which is the sum of yin and yang. When Wang Zongyue writes of the supreme ultimate being born from the limitless in *Shanxi Wang Zongyue's Taijiquan Treatise* (p. 11), he is saying that taiji (supreme limit) is born from wuji (no limit, or limitless). This is just one of the many ways that the Taiji fighters borrowed Taoist theory.

Taihang Mountains A Chinese mountain range in Shanxi Province. The name means "The Great Running Mountains."

Taihua Taihua Shan, or the Great Hua Peak ("Hua" means "magnificent"), is the southernmost and highest peak of Hua Mountain, located in Shaanxi Province. Hua Mountain is the western member of the Five Sacred Mountains and is an important center of Taoism. A temple was established there as early as the second century BCE and the mountain remained a prominent center of Taoist internal alchemy until modern times.

Taiyi Taiyi is an alternate name for the Zhongnan Mountains.

Tongguan A fortified mountain pass in Shaanxi Province south of the confluence of the Wei and Yellow Rivers. It was an important checkpoint protecting the capital city of Chang'an (present-day Xi'an). During the Tang Dynasty (618–907), the fall of Tongguan ("high pass") to rebels led directly to the capture of Chang'an. If the poet Xu Hun was at Tongguan in the poem, "On an Autumn Day, Inscribed at Tongguan Staging Post on My Way to the Capital" (p. 17), he would have been traveling from east to west and passing Hua Mountain on his way to Chang'an. Xu was not a healthy man, and so his longing for Hua Mountain, where methods of long life were studied, and his dream of being a fisherman or woodsman take on a poignant contrast to his career as an official.

Wencheng A district of Xianyang City, Shaanxi Province, just northwest of the modern city of Xi'an.

West Lake The West Lake is in the city of Hangzhou, Zhejiang Province. Considered one of the most beautiful places in China, the freshwater lake is divided by three causeways, and its shores are lined with temples, pagodas, and gardens. It influenced poets and painters throughout Chinese history.

Wu One of the states during the Western Zhou Dynasty (1046–771 BCE), Wu was founded in the eleventh century BCE and ended in 473 BCE. Wu was located at the mouth of the Yangzi River and east of the state of Chu.

Xian Mountain Its full name is Xiangyang ("High Yang") Mountain and it is located in Hubei Province.

Xiang River This is chief river draining Dongting Lake. The Xiang (the name is also an abbreviation for Hunan Province) is the largest river in Hunan Province. The river flows generally northeast through Guangxi and Hunan Provinces, and its tributaries reach into Jiangxi and Guangdong Provinces.

Xianjing Originally referring to the Qin capital of Xianyang. It is located in Shaanxi and is just west of Chang'an (now Xi'an). The term was also used to refer to Chang'an itself.

Xie, General Xie Shang (308–357) was a general stationed near Bull Island (a stopping place on the Yangzi near present-day Dangtu County, Anhui Province). One moonlit autumn night, he heard someone chanting poems while on a boat. It turned out to be a poet named Yuan Hong (328–376). The general invited the poet to board his own boat, and the two of them spent the night in delighted conversation. In "Recalling the Past during a Night-Mooring at Bull Island" (p. 30), Li Bai laments the absence of such a friend with whom he can discuss poetry.

Xie, Tutor Xie An (320–385) was a scholar and statesman of the Jin Dynasty (265–420). He was appointed overseer of imperial secretariat affairs after having served as minister of education. He oversaw the construction of a new palace in Jiankang and played a leading role in establishing a national university. Eventually, Xie became the prime minister. When the country was invaded by a large army, Xie organized seven armies in opposition. He was granted the posthumous title of senior mentor and is commonly addressed as Tutor Xie, as he was in Du Fu's poem, "Leaving the Grave of Grand Marshall Fang" (p. 37).

Xu, Lord This is a reference to a governor of Xuzhou (today, the fourth largest prefecture-level city of Jiangsu Province). Du Fu's reference in "Leaving the Grave of Grand Marshall Fang" (p. 37) depends on understanding Ji Zha (576–484 BCE). Ji Zha, descended from royalty, was a scholar, statesman, and diplomat. He is considered by some to be a sage equal in fame to Confucius. Once he visited Xuzhou on a diplomatic mission and the governor admired his sword. Ji Zha inwardly resolved to make a gift of his sword when his duties were complete. However, when he returned, the governor had already died. In great regret, Ji Zha hung his sword at the governor's grave.

Yan (state) An ancient state during the Zhou Dynasty (1046–256 BCE) from the eleventh century–221 BCE. Its capital eventually became the current capital city of Beijing.

Yan Mountain A mountain located in Gansu Province with a cave where the sun was thought to sink at night.

Yang Gate The full Chinese name is Yangguan. It was a fortified pass in what is now Duhuang County, Gansu Province, and it was an important landmark along the Silk Road. It was the westernmost administrative center of ancient China. When Wang Wei says farewell to his friend in "Seeing Yuan Er Off on a Mission to Anxi"(p. 8), he knows his friend is embarking on an uncertain and dangerous mission.

Yang, General Yang Hu (221–278) was a general of the Western Jin Dynasty (265–317). He was known for his humility and foresight. At first, he advocated the conquest of the rival state of Eastern Wu, but when that was not immediately possible, Yang sought détente with the Eastern Wu while he was stationed at the border region of Xiangyang. He impressed everyone with his kindness and goodwill. Years later, the people of Xiangyang built a monument for him on Mount Xian. Visitors wept so often upon reading of his benevolence that the monument became known as the Stela of Tears. This is the scene in "Climbing Xian Mountain Together with Friends" (p. 16), by Meng Haoran. The Jin finally conquered Eastern Wu in 280.

Yao, Emperor Traditionally believed to have lived c. 2356–2255 BCE, Yao was one of China's legendary rulers, and a member of a group called the Three Sovereigns and Five Emperors. He is held as a paragon of the sage-king.

Yellow River A river in northern China. Along with the Yangzi River, the Yellow River, or Huang He, is one of the two major rivers in China. It flows through nine provinces before emptying into the Bohai Sea off Shandong Province. Its basin is the birthplace of Chinese civilization.

Youzhou An ancient city in northern China and the capital of the State of Yan (eleventh century–222 BCE). It was located where the modern city of Beijing now stands. Youzhou ("Serene Prefecture") was an important commercial and military hub during the Tang Dynasty (618–907) when Chen Zi'ang wrote "Song of Climbing the Youzhou Terrace" (p. 70).

Yueyang Gate Tower With a name meaning "Mountain Sun," this tower is on the shore of Dongting Lake in Yueyang, Hunan Province. It's one of the three famous towers south of the Yangzi. Its three levels of roofs are covered in yellow tile and are said to look like a general's helmet.

Yuezhi An ancient people first reported as nomads living in the grasslands of present-day Gansu Province during the first millennium BCE. Over the centuries, they were a fundamental part of trade during the Silk Road. After centuries of war and migration, one branch of the Yuezhi settled in Tibet.

Zhongnan Mountains These mountains are a branch of the Qin Mountain Range in Shaanxi Province, south of the city of Xi'an. The Zhongnan ("End of the South") Mountains have been a popular place for Taoist as well as Buddhist recluses. The Complete Perfection Sect of Taoism was founded in the mountains. Since the mountains were close to Chang'an (Xi'an), disgraced officials often fled there to escape disgrace or punishment. See "Returning at Year's End to South Mountain" (p. 53) by Meng Haoran.

Zou A minor state that existed during the Zhou Dynasty (1046–256 BCE). It was conquered by King Xuan of Chu (r. 369–340 BCE). The state was located in the southwest of modern-day Shandong Province.

NOTES ON PRIMARY BIBLIOGRAPHIC SOURCES

Analects Known in Chinese as *Lunyu*, or *Edited Conversations*, this is a collection of sayings and ideas attributed to Confucius. The book was compiled by his followers in the Warring States era (475–221 BCE).

Book of Lord Shang Called *Shangjunshu*, this is a central book of the Legalism school of philosophy. Lord Shang was Gongsun Yang (390–338 BCE).

Book of Rites Known in Chinese as *Liji*, this collection of texts describes the social forms, administrative standards, and ceremonial rites of the Zhou Dynasty (c. 1046–256 BCE). The book was first compiled in the Warring States era (475–221 BCE) and was revised several times.

Classic of Poetry Known in Chinese as *Shijing*, this oldest collection of poetry dates from the eleventh–seventh centuries BCE and contains 305 poems. It is said to have been edited by Confucius.

Daodejing This book is one of the primary texts of Taoism and has become a part of world philosophy. It is also known as the *Tao Te Ching* (an earlier transliterated title) or referenced after its author's name as the *Laozi*. The name *Daodejing* literally translates to "Tao-Virtue-Classic," with the word *jing* or *classic* being the designation for a canonical work of Chinese culture. The book of roughly 5,000 words, divided into eighty-one chapters, is a fundamental text for both philosophical and religious Taoism, and it strongly influenced other schools, such as Legalism, Confucianism, and Chinese Buddhism, especially Chan or Zen Buddhism, which uses many Taoist words and concepts. Chinese poets, painters, calligraphers, and even garden designers have used the *Daodejing* as a source of inspiration. Its influence has also spread widely outside of Asia, and it is among the most translated works in world literature.

Yijing Also known as the *I Ching*, or the *Classic of Changes,* the *Yijing* is popularly labeled as a book of divination. While it can be used in that fashion, the book is really a repository of centuries of accumulated wisdom. The Eight Trigrams upon which it is based were created by Fu Xi (2852–2737 BCE) in the earliest stages of Chinese civilization. A feudal prince named Ji Chang, and posthumously known as King Wen (1152–1056 BCE), created one major section of the *Yijing* called "The Statement." One of his sons, the Duke of Zhou (Zhou Gong; eleventh century BCE), created commentaries for each line of the hexagrams called "The Lines." Confucius (551–479 BCE) himself is credited with writing "The Images," and these are the portions of the *Yijing* incorporated into this book. Later commentators added the *Ten Wings,* including the "Great Treatise." These sections explain various aspects of the *Yijing*.

Three Hundred Tang Poems This anthology was compiled about 1763 as *Tangshi Sanbai Shou*. The poems of the Tang Dynasty are considered to be the apex of Chinese poetry.

Shanxi Wang Zongyue's Taijiquan Treatise Written by Wang Zongyue (c. fifteenth century?) as *Shanyou Wang Zongyue Taijiquan Lun,* this work contains many of the key theories of the martial art, Taijiquan.

Sunzi's Art of Strategy *Sunzi Bingfa* is commonly known as *The Art of War*. This military treatise dates from the fifth century BCE. The book has remained one of the primary sources of strategy since then, and it has influenced military studies, business tactics, and legal strategy.

Mengzi This book was named after its author, Mengzi (372–289 BCE), whose named was Latinized as Mencius. He is considered the second most prominent Confucian philosopher after Confucius himself. The *Mengzi* is a collection of anecdotes and records of conversations between Mengzi and the rulers of several of the Warring States regarding moral and political philosophy.